W9-APB-484

THAT KELLY FAMILY

Other books by John McCallum

THE TIGER WORE SPIKES

DUMB DAN

THIS WAS FOOTBALL

HOW YOU CAN PLAY LITTLE LEAGUE BASEBALL

John McCallum

THAT KELLY FAMILY

A. S. Barnes and Company New York

Manufactured in the United States of America.

PUBLISHED ON THE SAME DAY IN THE DOMINION OF CANADA
BY THE COPP CLARK COMPANY, LTD., TORONTO.

LIBRARY OF CONGRESS CATALOG CARD NUMBER 56-10859

Dedication

To all those lion-hearted giants who have ever pulled an oar, whose eyes have felt the sting and sweat as they gave it "just 20 more," this book is affectionately dedicated.

(*NOTE:* John B. Kelly, Sr. is turning over his share of royalties derived from the sale of this book to amateur athletics.)

Preface

Watching Grace Kelly, a picture of exquisite beauty, move down the aisle of an ancient chapel on the arm of her handsome father, Jack Kelly, in April of 1956 to be wed to Prince Rainier of Monaco, I couldn't help but think of my old friend, Walter C. Kelly, the beloved "Virginia Judge" of vaudeville days.

How Walter's jovial, ruddy Irish face would have glowed with pride. *His* niece being given in holy matrimony—by his kid brother Jack—to a reigning European prince! The "Judge" undoubtedly would have bestowed a benevolent grin on the scene, and with a feeling of deep sincerity boomed —"THE LUCKY FELLOW."

Such was Walter Kelly's tremendous pride in his family.

It has been eighteen years since Walter passed away, and no doubt he has been treating the angels with his richly embellished accounts of the mighty Kelly achievements. It seems that it was only the day before yesterday that I sat in our golf club house listening to the "Judge's" mellow voice say as he raked in the poker chips:

"This is one of the few forms of exercise for which the Creator designed me. But he did bless me with a strong voice to cheer the boys on to win. Did I ever tell you guys what my kid brother Jack did in the Olympics?"

Not one of us in the poker game would make a protest. Even an oft-told story lost nothing in Walter's telling. He was a story-teller first of all, loquacious and rich with humorous anecdotes. Any funny story retold by the "Judge" was invariably funnier when he got through with it.

The Kelly kids have taken up where the old folk left off. Something exciting and successful is always happening to some member of this extraordinary family.

Kell, the only son of the Jack Kellys, has followed in his father's giant footsteps by winning scores of sculling medals and championships. And everybody who can read knows that Grace has become one of the most famous of all movie stars, enjoying world-wide popularity, and climaxing her breathtaking career by becoming the Princess of Monaco.

Writing the story of the fabulous Philadelphia Kellys would have been duck soup for John McCallum, a highly competent young man who is the author of four other books, if the "Virginia Judge" were still alive. Walter was the *talker* of the Kelly clan. Talking, in fact, was his business. It was also an art with Walter, the incomparable vaudeville monologist.

I will never forget the victory celebration Walter staged back in 1920 when Jack became the first American to win an Olympic sculling championship. That shindig will stand up against any Homeric or Gaelic event. The stories Walter told of his kid brother's prowess in sports were so gargantuan that I was awed beyond words, until Jack later tipped me off that Walter's yarns were more than slightly exaggerated. For a time there I regarded Jack as a cross between Babe Ruth, Jack Dempsey and Croesus.

A few years ago Jack and I collaborated in editing and rewriting Walter's autobiography (*Of Me I Sing*) which had been stashed away in a trunk after his untimely passing in 1939. Written in Walter's genial turn-of-the-century style, a language of gentle humor and graciousness we could well use today, the manuscript was so rich in theatrical lore, sporting reminiscences, and famous characters that we simply had to share this treasure with the rest of the world.

The late Grantland Rice, dean of sport writers, urged me to do something about getting the manuscript published. As a parting farewell to his old friend, Granny wrote the epilogue. George Ade contributed the Foreword. The book was a big hit, and Jack Kelly still receives requests for the book, though it has been out of print for three years.

(Editor's note: Some time later when Grace Kelly came out of the blue to rocket to movie fame, it was only natural that her father should call on Mr. Conlon to help guide and counsel her. As Pete Martin wrote in an article about Grace in *Saturday Evening Post:* "Scoop Conlon, a long-time friend of the Kellys', is in the public relations business out in Hollywood. He keeps a weather eye on Grace's career.")

Now that Grace has become one of the most famous women in the world, many people are under the impression that she was lucky as well as talented. To the contrary, in the early days of her Hollywood career she was faced with what appeared to be insurmountable obstacles. She has never been the Hollywood type of girl. When she first came out, she was shy, extremely reticent and serious-minded, yet well-poised, well-bred, and naturally modest. Few had her pegged as movie star material. One of the movie colony's most famous producers blandly predicted a quick fadeout for her.

But the quiet young lady from East Falls, Pennsylvania, had all the rare courage, grim determination and natural modesty that characterized her father and brother, champion oarsmen and born leaders; her Uncle George, Pulitzer Prize-winning playwright; and, of course, Uncle Walter. In a sense, Grace's victory in the annual Academy Award handout for her great performance in "The Country Girl"—and in only her second year, too!—matched the triumphs of the male Kellys.

The John B. (Jack) Kellys are strikingly individualistic. Jack's wife, Margaret, was a top model and cover girl in her youth, today a charming hostess and civic leader. Peggy, the oldest daughter, who is happily married and the mother of two little girls, has always been the apple of father Jack's eye. He swears that Peggy is the most talented member of the family. Lizanne, the youngest, also married and a mother, was a fine athlete, actress and campus leader at the University of Pennsylvania.

I have not attempted to touch on Jack's widely diversified achievements which have made the name John B. Kelly known and respected the world over, nor on his son's rowing achievements. John McCallum does that for you in the 75,000 words that follow.

That Kelly Family is a heart-warming saga of a remarkable family, founded in East Falls, Pennsylvania, by John Henry Kelly and Mary Ann Costello back in the post-Civil War years. If one were to select an ideal American family, it seems to me that the Jack Kellys would be a splendid choice because they represent what we admire in people—high principles as well as ambitions, modesty and sportsmanship as well as courage and determination to excel; clean living, religious people of tolerance, humor and decency.

The Kellys are truly All-Americans.

SCOOP CONLON

Contents

Dedication	v
Preface by Scoop Conlon	vii
Introduction by Bill Corum	xiii
Prelude In Verse	xvii
Mr. Philadelphia	3
The Early Years	13
"The Virginia Judge"	25
A Star Is Born	43
One Man In A Boat	57
All's Fair In Love & War	71
Kelly For Brickwork	83
A Dark Day	91
Jack's Prayers Answered	103
Margaret Gets Her Man	115
Second "Honeymoon"	119
The Political Years	125
Chip Off The Old Brick	137
"Hale America"	147
Bringing Up The Kellys	157
Poetic Justice	167
Homecoming	175
Grace Leaves Home	199
Oscar Night For Grace	209
Life Rolls On	215
Index	225

Introduction

We talk about the people who are "the preservers of civilization," "the backbone of the country," "the hope of the future" —all the other stock phrases that imply safety and progress. Sometimes we put the laurel wreath on one set of brows, sometimes on another. But deep in our hearts we know that the present security and the future of our nation always have hinged on The Great American Family; families like that of the Philadelphia Kellys, for example.

The story of the Kellys reads a bit like Merriwell out of Horatio Alger, almost fictional in its telling, but any way you cut it, the saga of this extraordinary clan is as factual as a calendar.

I have known John B. (Jack) Kelly, Sr. for about twenty years. For the last half-dozen years I urged him to authorize someone to write a book about him and his family, because the life and times of the Kellys have been too extraordinary to be lost. I was happy to see them reclaimed here.

I think the Kellys of this generation are, as were their forebears, an exaggeration of most of the admirable qualities we like to find in a family. They are an energetic, rugged and unyielding lineage, slaves to their own strict standards. The Kellys long have been about as conspicuous as Philadelphia's 30th Street Pennsylvania Station, which, like about seventy-five per cent of the city's important office buildings, bears the credit: Brickwork by Kelly.

It was George Ade, the playwright and author, who once said, "Some biographer . . . should write a book entitled 'The Kelly Boys.' Their parents must have been remarkable people. Each of their sons became a celebrity in his own right."

There were six Kelly boys, but of these I was closest to the late Walter, the beloved "Virginia Judge" of vaudeville days.

Walter Kelly, often compared with Mark Twain and Will Rogers as a humorist, was labeled prince of raconteurs and graduate cum laude of dialects. But he was also a great pal of the sports crowd. He golfed with John J. McGraw and Judge Kenesaw Mountain Landis, pursued wily tarpon and sailfish with Tex Rickard, and hobnobbed with James J. Corbett.

Once Walter and George Ade played a round of golf at Sarasota, Florida. One of the tees faced a water hazard. Walter promptly dunked two balls into the water. Turning to his caddie, a Negro lad, he asked for a "floater" ball. The youth took a shiny Silver King from the bag. Walter eyed the ball and said, "Be sure it's a floater."

"I sho' will," replied the caddie. Whereupon he walked to the edge of the water hole and dropped the ball in eight feet of water. Watching it disappear, the kid turned to Walter and said, "No, suh, she won't float."

Walter was one of the greatest story tellers of his or any other era, and one of his favorite tales concerned two Irish fishermen who were out in an open boat off the coast of

Queenstown. "A sudden storm came up and swept them to sea," related Walter. "Darkness was closing in and there was no sight of land. It was pouring rain. The situation seemed hopeless. One of the fishermen dropped to his knees and began to pray.

" 'Oh, God,' he pleaded, 'if ever I get out of this I'll go to church every Sunday, I'll never take another drink, I'll quit gambling, I will never go out with another. . . .' "

" 'Hold it, Martin!' cried his partner. 'Don't commit yourself! I think I see land.' "

Like Bobby Jones in golf, my good friend Jack Kelly, the central figure in this story, was the "grand slam" man of rowing. He won every race in which he rowed during 1919–1920. He remains the only American to win the Olympic Games single sculls, and the only one in the world to win the single and doubles in the same Olympics.

As president and general manager of Churchill Downs, I have had much occasion to be with Jack these past few years, he being president of Atlantic City Race Track, one of his many sidelines. Jack never has owned a race horse, but he cut down the first tree on the meadows at Atlantic City in 1946, and since has watched it grow into one of the finest tracks in America.

I think the nicest accolade given Jack Kelly was that uttered by Dr. Patrick O'Callaghan, the wealthy strong boy from Ireland. Some years ago Dr. O'Callaghan toured the United States putting on wrestling exhibitions. At a luncheon in Philadelphia, he was asked why a man of his professional stature mixed with the grapplers.

"Because," he said, "I feel this is the best way I can help my country and my people, by going out into the sports world and demonstrating how high Irish values are. I am, let me say, like your Jack Kelly. All over the world your Mr.

Kelly made people admire and respect American values, American courage, strength, ability, and decision. That's what I want to do for Ireland."

No one has practiced high ideals harder than Kelly.

He never has stopped being a champion.

BILL CORUM

Prelude in Verse

TO AN OARSMAN

by Jack Kelly

Have you heard the old call that comes to us all
To get out in the fields and the air;
To shove into a heap the letters that keep
You chained fast to your desk and your chair?

Do you know the delight of a still moonlight night,
As your paddle flashes and gleams,
And you see the big moon rising up o'er the gloom
Of the pines, where your campfire beams?

Have you set out decoys, to learn all the joys,
Of the whir and the incoming swing
Of the blue-bills or teal as you see them to wheel
And come in with dropped foot and set wing?

Have you straightened your kinks on an eighteen-hole links,
Do you know the champagne of a drive

That lifts the ball true, a white speck in the blue,
That rises, then carries, then dives?

If you've answered the call, you've perhaps tried them all,
And others besides, for they're more;
But tell me, my friend, 'ere I come to the end,
Have you pulled out your heart at an oar?

Have you sat at the line, with cold chills down your spine,
Just before a hard race had begun,
When each movement intense seems a year of suspense
While you watch for the flash of the gun?

Have you seen your own sweep, as you swing, seem to creep
Past the boat that's not ten yards away,
While you tighten your grip, as the oars flash and rip
With a swirl through the water and spray—

And your eyes sting with sweat, and you fight hard to get
Your next breath, and your tongue's like a bone;
Have you given her ten and then done it again,
When you're rowing on pure nerve alone?

Have you dropped with the gun, just knowing you've won,
While you grin to yourself if you can?
If you have, here's my hand, for it takes "guts" and sand;
It's a game that was built for a man.

THAT KELLY FAMILY

Mr. Philadelphia

Long ago, according to Irish legend, there lived in County Wexford, Ireland, a laughing, valiant giant of a warrior named John Kelly. In 1798, the year of The Great Rebellion, he led a tiny knot of men along a lonely country road from Taghmon to Wexford and trapped and captured The Meath Militia.

After this show of valor and raw courage, the name of John Kelly spread throughout the land and his legion of worshippers began to call him "The Dauntless Kelly of Killan," singing of his gallantry in verse:

"Tell me, who is the giant
With gold curling hair,
He who rides at the head of your band?
Seven feet is his height

With some inches to spare
And he looks like a king in command.

Ah, my lads that the pride
Of the bold Shemaliers
'Mong our greatest of heroes—a man!
Fling your beavers aloft
And give three ringing cheers
For John Kelly, the boy from Killan."

For centuries the Irish family name of Kelly has played no small part in world history, with all their struggles, hardships, adventures, successes, and rare humor. The Kellys originally were one of the most powerful clans in Connaught, where, as chiefs of Ui Maine, they ruled in Galway and Roscommon.

The Kellys always have been proud of their fighting heritage, proud, for example, of the 695 clan members who fought in General Washington's army during the Revolutionary War. The Kelly clan has lived up to its warlike patronymic wherever it has emigrated—across hills, mountains, rivers, great oceans, to the far corners of the world . . . to East Falls, Pennsylvania, U.S.A.

To find a modern counterpart of "The Dauntless Kelly of Killan," you have only to look to East Falls, Pennsylvania, in northwest Philadelphia, for three score and seven years the home of John Brendan (Jack) Kelly, a handsome, vigorous man who won himself a corner of sporting history by his great rowing feats in the '20s. Behind Jack Kelly is the story of the rise of a remarkable Irish-American family, of men and women blessed with strong arms and good looks, a dogged instinct for hard work, and a sure feel for success.

Jack's oldest brother, Patrick Henry, rose from carpet mill apprentice, to bricklayer, labor organizer, and finally a contractor. He built the huge Free Library on Philadelphia's beautiful Parkway, Pennsylvania's Capitol Annex at Harrisburg, and many imposing churches and schools.

Next came brother Walter, known the world over as the beloved "Virginia Judge." He too started a youthful career in the carpet mills nearby. In turn he became a machinist, candidate for Congress, hotel keeper, and then one of the world's greatest monologists.

Then there is the Pulitzer Prize winner George Kelly. He became an apprentice draftsman and studied at night school. The stage finally claimed him, and after serving in World War I he turned to writing full-length plays. *Craig's Wife* and *The Show Off* quickly brought him huge success.

A fourth brother, Charles Vincent, who died last January at seventy-six, was also a graduate from the carpet mills. From bricklayer he rose to contractor. He reached fame as a crack runner, football, and basketball player.

In spite of the high goal set by his older brothers, Jack Kelly has managed to do pretty well by himself and the name of Kelly. But imaginative as boys are in erecting their marvelous castles in the sky, could Jack, as a small boy, ever in his wildest flight of fancy have some day seen himself a wealthy contractor, president of a company that helped to build the United Nations Building, New York's Radio City and Coliseum, in addition to many other fabulous structures across the country? Or the greatest American oarsman who ever lived? An important fixture in politics and public life and recently named, with his son, John B. Jr., to the Helms Hall of Fame?

Could he have foreseen having a son who would go on to twice win the Diamond Sculls, the English Classic? And a daughter who would cop Hollywood's Oscar Award and marry a prince? Folly. Not even in a person's dizziest day dreams do these things happen. Yet all of these things—and much more—have happened to Jack Kelly, making a true story that has become an inspiration to all Americans, both young and old.

The citizens of Philadelphia did themselves much honor in the spring of 1955 when they gave Jack Kelly a testimonial banquet, and from the bottom of their hearts tendered him a grateful ovation for all that he means to them.

You can't go anywhere in Philadelphia without feeling the influence of the man. Among numerous other projects, Jack created the first municipally-operated tent theatre, the Playhouse in the Park, and Fairmount Park directors named their Olympic swimming pool after him. It is estimated that Kelly For Brickwork, Inc. is responsible for seventy-five per cent of Philadelphia's office buildings. When Jack stands at the Philadelphia Post Office, his brick buildings are all around him, including the *Evening Bulletin* and 30th Street railroad station.

When they gave Jack the 1955 Humanitarian Award, they were telling him, in effect, "Thanks, Jack Kelly. Thank you for being such a big part of us." Nobody ever will know how many people have received aid of one sort or another from Jack, or how many acts of kindness and generosity he has performed for the budding athletes of Philadelphia. Where there are debts of gratitude, he doesn't keep books.

Jack, for many years, has had the milkman and breadman on the East Falls route report to him any signs of impoverishment. If they hear of a family needing economic aid—one that is earnestly attempting to make ends meet but can't—they tell Jack about it. Jack takes the ball from there, running interference for the family until it can get back on its feet. Times without number he has contributed to charity, resolutely rejecting any credit.

Sitting at his desk one morning, Jack ran across an item in the paper about a little Philadelphia girl who was paralyzed from the waist down. Her parents were poor. There was no money to buy a wheelchair. Jack called the treasurer of his company into his office.

"Miss Mullin," he said, "here's $100. Give it to the girl's mother and tell her to buy a wheelchair. Don't tell her where the money came from."

To this day, the girl's parents have no idea who paid for the wheelchair.

If there is one thing that characterizes Jack, it is consideration of others. Take his loyalty and devotion to his employees, for example. He has established a retirement pension plan for them. He owns fifty-one per cent of his company's stock, providing for his employees to share in the other forty-nine per cent.

Jack hovers over his staff in watchdog fashion, behaving toward some like a boy scout leader, toward others like a tough army sergeant. If his employees are troubled, they come in and talk it over with "John B." Jack can usually find the solution for impending divorce, bankruptcy, medical repairs, failing grades, overweight or the baby-sitter problem.

After Grace's engagement to Prince Rainier III, ruler of the tiny principality of Monaco, was publicly announced, a columnist called Jack and asked him what his reaction was to the engagement. Jack answered, "We're not impressed by royalty. We're impressed by the man. Marriage is not a game of musical chairs with us. We play for keeps."

The popular conception of a president of a big business (and Jack now owns the country's biggest brick construction company) does not fit the old sculling champion, with his warm, friendly manner, his blunt, shining features and his manner of going directly to the point. Jack is quite different from the gimlet-eyed, 16-inch-gun type of executive who shuts himself off from his hired hands by living in an ivory tower.

Jack is the only bricklaying employer to hold a gold union card, voted at the Bricklayers' Convention in 1920. He still cherishes his lifetime membership card and attends meetings. When, at one such, a fellow lodge brother yelled, "Throw him out," Jack calmly stood up and said, "If the gentleman who said that will step up and try, I'll be glad to accommodate him." The matter was quickly dropped.

Thirty-six years have passed since Jack won his first Olympic title, but he remains as straight as a ramrod, lean and sinewy, with the spirit of a man who won the world's championship only the day before yesterday. He is slightly heavier, ten pounds, but there is still a gladiator quality about him. His sense of humor—and he laughs often—the impish wit that so few of our champions ever have had, is still with him. He is a handsome man, with skin tanned to the color of varnished cedar and accentuated by a broad toothpaste-ad smile. He is a splendid example of elderly manhood. Even now his gait and posture is a model of grace and rhythm.

Westbrook Pegler, seeing Jack and his son, Kell, at a sports banquet in New York a couple of years ago, wrote in his syndicated column the following day: "Unquestionably, the champions are special. There is a style and a look to them. They wear greatness as a habit. Were you to see the Jack Kellys, of Philadelphia, father and son, the scullers, you could no more mistake them for ordinary men than a cart-horse for a thoroughbred . . . I feel a little ashamed to carry on like this. Something just came over me. I will be myself again tomorrow."

Jack Dempsey still likes to tell about the first time he ever saw Jack Kelly. It was at Atlantic City, on the beach, just after the First World War.

"Kelly was about twenty-seven, stood a half inch taller and weighed a few pounds more than I," recalled the old heavyweight champion. "He had broader shoulders, but a smaller waist. I never saw a finer specimen of a man. In the length and breadth of America there was no finer body. He was wearing swim trunks. I was strongly impressed by his physique and started to inquire about him. Finally a mutual friend introduced us. I asked Jack if he knew anything about boxing, and he said, 'Sure, enough to protect myself against some of these champions fighting today.' "

Dempsey broke into a smile.

"You know," he said, "I'm still trying to figure out what he meant."

Another former heavyweight champion, Gene Tunney, always has held Kelly in similar esteem. Tunney won the AEF light-heavyweight title during World War I by taking a decision in the tournament finals from the same man Kelly knocked out in the first round in a fight two months before. A broken ankle, suffered in a truck accident, prevented Kelly from fighting for the championship.

Kelly and Tunney always have been warm friends, occasionally getting together for dinner. One night Jack told Gene, "You know, it was a good thing we never met in the ring."

"Why?" asked Gene.

"If I hadn't broken my ankle," said Jack, "you wouldn't have won the AEF title, and maybe you wouldn't have gone on to win the world's championship."

Later, to another friend, Tunney said, "And for all I know, Kelly may have beaten me or anybody, if he set himself to the job. He was a very determined fellow with a rugged constitution, and he usually got what he went after." Kelly and Tunney are continually ribbing each other in their frequent letters.

Home training had much to do with Jack's success, besides his sound soul and spirit, but his early habits were greatly responsible. Habits formed in youth are apt to last through later life. Jack's have. He never has made a parade of his virtues. He merely lives the way he likes to live—decently, soberly, bravely. He's a living example of the Greek slogan: *"In mens sana in corpore sano,"* a clean mind in a healthy body. The Golden Age of Greece knew how to admire the simple virtues, too.

Over the years Jack has given more than $200,000 to Philadelphia's sports for youth movement. When it concerns kids and athletics, Jack never asks, "How much is it going to cost me?" He says simply, "Go ahead and do it—if you think it is good for the kids—and send me the bill."

Jack contributes annually upwards of $20,000 to the city's rowing program. Right now he is planning a Rowing Hall of Fame, similar to the baseball shrine at Cooperstown. When his heavy schedule allows, he also gets out with Kell and personally tutors Philadelphia's junior oarsmen.

"There are many things to remember about rowing," he tells them. "One of them is to keep in good shape all year around. It's getting back in shape for rowing that takes it out of you."

Physical fitness is Jack's favorite subject, and when he gets wound up on it the Stars and Stripes leap out and light up the heavens.

In the field of physical education, Margaret Kelly, Jack's wife, also is an acknowledged authority, full of the soundest sort of common sense. She is her own best testimonial to her teachings. At fifty-seven, she looks almost as young as her daughters. Even yet, when down at the beach, she will arise with the sun, take a swim, then ride a bicycle up and down the beach. Exercise, she testifies, keeps her trim. She also has said—and who can dispute this?—that too many athletes make the mistake of letting themselves grow fat during the off-season and then taking the weight off violently in preseason training.

"The secret of staying in good physical condition is simply a matter of regular living," she says. "I hate to think what the Kelly house would have been like if God hadn't given Kell the physique, the temperament and the competitive fire to be a champion oarsman. Having our son choose rowing was something Jack had his heart on almost from the day the boy was born. He didn't talk about it a great deal at first, but it was there."

Kell, come to think of it, is one of the very few really top-flight figures in sports who went beyond his father's most far-flung vision and ambition. Bobby Feller is another. But how often does it work out? When does a Ty Cobb beget a Cobb, Bobby Jones a Jones, Babe Ruth a Ruth, Red Grange a Grange, Jack Dempsey a Dempsey, Gene Tunney a Tunney, . . . and so forth? Still fathers will always try—dreaming and hoping they will be half as fortunate as John B. Kelly.

The Early Years

Like his older brothers, Pat, Walter and George, Jack Kelly, the central figure of this book, had many interests beside learning a trade during his formative years. He was all boy. He loved sports. Had you asked him to name the greatest man in the world, he would not have hesitated a second.

"Fred Sheppard, he's the greatest," young Jack would have told you, even though the newspapers of those days occasionally mentioned other prominent names, such as Teddy Roosevelt and John L. Sullivan and Henry Ford and John J. McGraw and Thomas Edison.

Fred Sheppard of Harlem, New York, you understand, was the greatest oarsman of his era, a national champion, and in the worshipful eyes of the Kelly boy, he was just one cut below Sainthood. Mr. Sheppard was a sort of God who moved through a kind of golden haze in which his soiled flannel robe seemed pure white.

As a boy of ten, Jack Kelly posed in the role of opportunity knocking at the gates of the Schuylkill Navy's Boathouse Row, located near the Kelly home. More than anything, the youngster wanted to learn how to row, to be a champion sculler some day. He wanted to emulate the masterful Fred Sheppard.

Without fail, Jack rented a bicycle for fifteen cents an hour and followed the boats on race days. The racing course was a mile and a half long, but the distance never discouraged Jack. The program generally consisted of eight races, and Jack, who cycled along the river bank adjacent to the competing shells, followed each event from start to finish, covering about twenty-five miles for the afternoon.

Jack loved those tall, muscular oarsmen. He tagged after them everywhere. After school hours, he'd hurry to the river and wistfully watch them take their practice spins. And when they returned to the boathouse, he stood a respectful distance away, and just hero-worshiped. No doubt about it, that was the life for young John Brendan Kelly. He loved the smell, the very atmosphere, of a boathouse. It had a unique aroma, compounded of perspiration, unlaundered gym clothing, rubbing alcohol, and countless other odors impossible to identify. Everywhere he gaped burly oarsmen were doing leg exercises, flexing their muscles, shadow boxing, and dancing around to loosen up. They were grunting, they were gritting, and they obviously doted on this way of life.

Years later, Jack Kelly was to ask himself: What is there about rowing that makes it different from other games? It's a trying, cussed, back-breaking sport, not at all glamorous in contrast to baseball, football and basketball. Why is it, then, that without any compulsion or inducement of any kind, day after day, men slip on sweat suits, grab an oar, and labor away on the river? It has been going on for a long time. There must be something very elemental about it. But Jack wasn't asking himself *why* he wanted to be an oarsman. He only knew that he yearned to be out there with the giants of the Schuylkill.

From this beginning, Jack, as a youth, found out for himself how much can be gained through the medium of genuine hero worship. He set out to match his heroes, assuring himself that if you have your own hero, and he is worth worshiping, then he must be worth trying to equal.

By trading on the natural mimicry inherent in all children, Jack would worm himself into a practice shell, when no one in the boathouse was looking, and imitate his idol, Fred Sheppard, tugging away on an oar.

To keep in physical form, Jack also played football and baseball and basketball. He swam and boxed. There were no recreation centers, boys' clubs or Y.M.C.A.'s in East Falls, Pennsylvania, in those days, so Jack and his teammates improvised their own games without much equipment.

There was a roadhouse nearby, called the Fairmount Inn, where the carriage trade stopped for refreshments. Sailor Tom Sharkey, contender for the heavyweight boxing title of the world, once trained at the Inn for a bout in Philadelphia. It developed into a popular training camp after that. Great pugilists like Terrible Terry McGovern, Battling Nelson and Gus Ruhlin made Fairmount Inn their Philadelphia hangout.

Jack Kelly and his playmates spent much of their spare time at the Inn. The customers sponsored junior boxing tournaments, putting up as much as five dollars in prize money to the winners. That represented a lot of spending money to the kids, and Jack recalls losing his first two fights attempting to win some of it. Then he did some deep thinking. He finally concluded that he would have to start training like the professionals. Soon he joined the older fighters in roadwork, toughening his legs and improving his wind.

Hughie McGovern, brother of Terrible Terry, the champion, was attracted by Jack's eagerness and determination. He gave the boy boxing lessons. In less than a month Jack won his first tournament.

Beaming from ear to ear, Jack walked into his home after the victory and handed his mother $4.75. Mary Kelly, a woman of high principles, did not approve of her son earning money with his fists. She said that the boy should give it back, but Jack's father, John Henry Kelly, came to the rescue. He convinced his wife that every boy should know how to protect himself. Mary Kelly relented. Jack kept the money.

It would be next to impossible to write about the life and times of Jack Kelly without liberally mentioning his mother. Ever since he was old enough to think seriously about anything, he thought what a tragic experience it would be if ever he lost his mother. Not that he didn't love his father, too, because he did, but his mother, like most mothers, was the one central figure in the family. She was the one who bore the brunt of all her youngsters' trials and afflictions, the one who seemed to smooth out all problems and ease all pain. It was she who steered them right and no matter how hard the world around them became, they knew they could always go to her, sure of being comforted.

Mary Costello Kelly was born in 1852 in Ireland, moving to England three years later. When she was only eight she was brought to America to live with her grandmother and aunt at Rutland, Vermont. That was in 1860. The little red school house she was enrolled in was located a mile down the road from her home.

"The school had a janitor," recalled Jack, "but my mother said that she felt he must have been something of a hibernating animal. On many a cold winter morning, after wading through a mile of snow drifts, she, along with some of the other pupils, gathered up shavings and kindlings and made a fire to warm the building and keep themselves from freezing.

"Mother said she guessed it would be that way all through life. There would always be some people who would do their share, and some who would do *two* shares. But the slackers, she said, weren't so smart as they thought they were. They were cheating themselves, if they only knew it, for there's no kind of work that won't teach you something."

Jack's father arrived in the United States from County Mayo, Ireland, in 1867 at the age of twenty. He had sailed across the Atlantic on a boat named the "City of Boston," which, ironically, was lost on its return voyage to Europe.

John Henry Kelly and Mary Costello were married in 1869. He was twenty-two, she seventeen. They began married life in Rutland, where the first of ten children, Patrick Henry, so named because of the intense patriotism of his father and mother, was born. The family later moved to Mineville, New York, birthplace of the second oldest, Walter, later to become known all over the world as "The Virginia Judge," a figure as familiar in the London drawing rooms as he was in the theatres of New York and Johannesburg, South Africa. An offer of a better job took the John Henry Kellys back to Vermont a year later again, and four more children (Anne, John, who later died of sunstroke when he was ten, Charles and Mary) joined Patrick Henry and Walter. From Vermont the Kellys moved to Philadelphia, settling down permanently, and bringing Elizabeth, George, Jack and Grace into the world.

When the family arrived in Philadelphia, the first thing Mary Kelly did was to go and touch the Liberty Bell. She always called America "God's country."

While some historians have given the Philadelphia Kellys a suggestion of brogue, actually they are about as American as Bunker Hill, Valley Forge, the Rocky Mountains, or the

Dakota Prairies. Mary Costello Kelly knew nothing about Ireland, only what she had read or heard. If you check, you will discover that the Kellys' forebears have been in this country for a hundred and twenty-five years. Both of Jack's great-grandmothers are buried in Vermont, also a great-great-grandmother.

Though John Henry Kelly started his career as a laborer, by the time Jack appeared the Kellys were a very comfortably circumstanced family. George Kelly, in reconstructing some of the family background for me, wrote in a letter that some of his earliest recollections of his youth include a picture of the latest sports model car standing in front of the Kelly home waiting to whisk Jack off to some sort of affair.

John and Mary Kelly, said George, both appreciated and knew good living—and knew how to provide it. John Henry Kelly was a powerful man. He stood six feet, weighed 200 pounds, hard as nails, yet was an extremely quiet man, very much the intellectual. Possessed with an uncanny memory, he could memorize poems of great length practically overnight. He once recited, verbatim, Thomas Moore's "Lalla Rookh," the Irish classic of some two hundred pages, while taking a casual stroll through the park one Sunday. At the time of his death, in 1917, he had risen to the point where he was recognized as one of Philadelphia's leading insurance men.

Jack's mother governed the pattern of her life with the soundest sort of philosophy. A friend of hers, a neighbor lady, asked her one time, "Mrs. Kelly, are you like most mothers?"

Mrs. Kelly didn't understand the question.

"I mean," explained her friend, "do you have a little more love for your boys than for your daughters?"

Jack's mother drew herself up.

"That's no question to put to a mother," she replied, finally. "But since you asked I will tell you the truth. There's a great

pride in the love I have for my sons, God bless them. But there's a special tenderness and understanding in my heart for my girls. The time to teach a child to respect you, as well as to love you, is before he has found that anything else is possible. The biggest battle is fought then, but the campaign of training goes on for many years. Do you know what the trouble is in most families?"

"No, Mrs. Kelly."

"The trouble is that in most families the mother is *afraid* of her children," said Jack's mother. "I never stood in fear of mine, even though I would have given my heart's blood for them. They are the whole world to me. But I've never been afraid of them. Why should I be? As children, I had more knowledge and experience and judgment than they had. For their own good, they must be taught to respect me as their superior. Not that I demand their respect just because I happen to be their mother. You can demand a *show* of respect, as long as you are the stronger. But the thing itself must be *earned*. I will never stop trying to earn the respect of my children."

Mary Kelly was as proud as a peacock of her children. They were, even if she did say so herself, fine young people—noisy, and a little too enthusiastically original, at times, but genuine and faithful and good-natured, and such a joy to have around the house. Each had individual complexities, of course, needing pulling or pushing occasionally, but Mary Kelly always seemed to know what to say and what to do to straighten them out. She was indeed a mature woman, psychologically and spiritually, with a gift of almost prophetic wisdom—a wise and capable ruler, had she been born in other circumstances.

Jack's parents taught their children a way of life that is as American as freedom itself: Be just and be punctual. Buy only what you need and make every effort to pay cash. Be sparing of promises, but once one is made keep it at all costs.

Jack and his brothers and sisters were made to understand two things about money. First, that every dollar, and every penny, represented somebody's labor. If a child had a dollar to spend, it meant that somebody had worked hard to earn that dollar, and that somebody had worked to save it. It didn't just drop out of the skies, like in a fairy tale.

Though Mary Kelly disliked personal publicity, she did permit *American Magazine* to feature her in an article in 1924, titled, "Oh, There Ought To Be A Million Mothers Like Mary Kelly." The writer who interviewed her wanted to know how it was possible to teach children a sound philosophy about money matters when they were still so young.

Mary Kelly said, "They can begin by doing little things to help around the house. You can easily make them understand that when they do one thing they are earning the right to do something else. Each of my youngsters, from the time he was able to toddle, has had some regular bit of work to do. It is each one's share in helping to supply our plain needs. If one of them wants something extra, he, or she, must do extra work to earn it. I try to show them what it means to have the things they want."

Jack Kelly is a multi-millionaire today, and could probably buy the factory, but there was a time in his boyhood when the most precious thing he could own was a new pair of ice skates. He remembers asking his mother to buy them for him. Studying the healthy eagerness on her son's upturned face, she thought to herself, Now, I mean he shall have those skates. 'Twill be good for him to be getting fine exercise out of doors. And 'twill make him very happy, too. But, first, I want him to learn the value of the money it will cost to buy them.

"Son," she said, "I want you to listen very closely. If you

want those skates badly enough, you will have to work extra for them. You will have to earn them."

Jack agreed.

"A growing boy like you must learn appreciation," she added. "I want you to go to the public library and find out all you can about those skates: what they are made of, how the iron has been dug out of the mines by hard-working men, and the wood has come from the forests, and the leather has once been the skin of some animal. I want you to see that a pair of skates has been earned for you by the labor of others, and that you must put your labor in it, too, if you want to enjoy them."

It sounded like a fair enough price to pay, and Jack, experiencing the exultation that comes with a challenge, dashed off to the library. He devoted his after school hours in the days that followed to reading all the books he could find relating to the forests, leather and steel. At home, his mother asked him questions, testing him on his research. When she was sure that he had thoroughly covered the subject, *then* she went down to the store and bought the skates for him.

Mary Kelly trained her children not only to have a sense of individual responsibility, but also to realize the need of mutual responsibility and helpfulness. When her oldest son, Patrick Henry, who was a born builder, had become a skilled brickmason and began to yearn for his own business, he saw an opportunity to acquire enough capital to start a company of his own. Seems that a Philadelphia newspaper was sponsoring a contest to determine the most popular employee in the city. The prize was a $5000 house. To win, the contestant had to compile the biggest total of voting coupons which were being featured daily in the paper.

Pat told his mother that if he could win that house he could sell it and use the money to start his own business.

"And why shouldn't you win it?" asked his mother. "It's the ballots that will win, not popularity. And you will have the ballots."

Whereupon she organized her offspring into a sort of flying squadron. Jack, then quite a good-sized boy, was assigned to get up before daybreak the first morning, follow the paper carrier on his rounds, and list the names of all subscribers to the sponsoring newspapers. This list was then apportioned among Jack's brothers and sisters. That very afternoon they went out and called at the various homes and repeated over and over their request:

"Please, ma'am, will you give me your vote for my brother?"

This plan was followed daily during the next couple of weeks. Mrs. Kelly, a master psychologist, armed each youngster with a small pair of scissors, which were always in evidence when the young Kellys uttered their plea for coupons. Few indeed could resist those scissors.

Pat easily won the contest, sold the house, set up his own company, and began to bid on contracts. He put his sister, Mary, who had just finished a college business course, in charge of his office, and made Charles, his younger brother, superintendent of the outside crew. The P. H. Kelly Building Company was on its way, inevitably becoming one of the most important building companies in the East. Many of Pennsylvania's most imposing structures are monuments to the achievements of P. H., who died in 1937.

Jack's father insisted that all of the Kelly boys learn a skilled trade. For example, George, as a result of his aptitude for higher mathematics, was being groomed for a career as a civil engineer when, like many young men in their teens, he felt that perhaps he should be a writer. He was correct in that conclusion, as the world was to see in the twenties, going on to become one of the leading dramatists and directors of the New York stage.

Talking to Jack, his sister, Mary, and judging from the tone of George's recollections, I couldn't help but feel that the happy moments far outnumbered the unhappy ones in the Kelly home. They made their own fun. Their mother always said that her family had more laughs than it was entitled to.

Walter and George and the baby of the family, Grace, were simply born for the stage. They were extremely witty, and blessed with warm humor. Grace, the pride of the Kellys, developed into a polished mimic. She had the Scotch dialect down so pat that Scotch friends insisted that she was Scotch, not Irish. She sang Harry Lauder songs dressed in kilts and tied the family in knots with her pleasantly comical funmaking. She was well on her way to star billing in the theatre before an untimely heart attack claimed her in her early twenties.

George Kelly outwardly appeared to be a very serious and conservative young man, but around his family he was the funniest man in the world—a facet of his character he kept well hidden from the public.

One of his favorite forms of tomfoolery was to bolt into the house, snatch a cloth from the table, sling it around his shoulders, and stalk up and down the living room, acting a scene from some play or other. Once, when his mother was trying to talk, she told him to keep quiet. Striking a Shakespearian pose, George retorted, "Go ahead and hurt me, but you will be sorry when my name is in lights." George doesn't remember ever having made any such remark, but brother Jack and sister Mary confirmed the incident and said it became a standard joke at home.

The Kellys knew how to laugh—*with,* as well as *at,* themselves.

"The Virginia Judge"

In early America, particularly during the Gaslight Era, families linked hands to work and play together. Warm companionship developed through striving toward the same goal. This spirit of all for one and one for all became a firm anchor to happiness for the Kellys.

While Walter Kelly, in his autobiography, *Of Me I Sing*, was glamorized as something of a former burlesque comedian, the dispenser of a lot of old-time jokes, those who knew him best feel that he did himself a grave injustice. His brother, George, points out that Walter was a celebrity at thirty years of age and looked it.

The Pulitzer Prize-winning playwright explained, "If there was ever a man of impeccable taste in the matter of his personal grooming, it was Walter. My mother was constantly deploring his extravagance in clothes. Though the vaudeville of his day is hardly understood by present-day readers, Walter was a man of dignity and good taste, certainly not a burlesque comedian. He became a star of the international stage, appearing in the English-speaking capitals and great cities of the world. He also appeared as a featured player in many legitimate attractions."

Walter was kind of a boyhood idol with Jack. When he stopped off at home between theatre engagements, he loved to entertain the Kellys with his hilarious stories and imitations, sending the family and neighbors into paroxysms of laughter. Gather Walter, George and Grace together in the same room, and it was a production worthy of the old Orpheum Circuit. Elizabeth, the sharpest of all in repartee, kept the others in line with her good-natured criticism, and Mary, with her barbed retorts, balanced off the overenthusiastic.

While, as George testified, Walter enjoyed deep respect and love in show business, he was a page right out of Mark Twain during his teen-age years. A sense of humor was alive in him. He just sort of reached out and plucked life, the way others pluck feverishly at apples on a tree.

Walter was only about eighteen the time his mother, out doing some shopping, noticed a crowd of maybe 500 people gathered on a street corner. She stopped to investigate. Imagine her surprise when she discovered that they were listening to her young son, Walter, standing atop a soap box, delivering a *political* speech.

Mother Kelly smiled to herself. "I have my doubts about it being good politics," she told herself, "but I'll grant it is a good speech."

The fact that Walter seldom missed a theatre engagement, was always on cue, can probably be attributed to the influence of his mother. She constantly lectured to him about promptness. "Nobody has a right to be late," she told him.

"Did you ever try to think of what would happen if everybody was unpunctual for a single day? Before nightfall the whole world would be in a tangle which only the good God Himself could straighten out. You must learn to feel a responsibility about this."

Some nights later Walter got permission to go out, promising his mother that he would be back at nine o'clock.

"Then you be back here at nine, even if you have to run a mile," commanded his mother. "God made darkness for sleep. The forces of evil are working after midnight."

To make a short story shorter, Walter was five or so minutes late coming back. His mother was waiting at the door for him as he bolted into the house. A southpaw, she wore a heavy gold wedding ring on her left hand, and she reached out and tapped the tardy Walter a solid thump on the side of the head with that armored left hand as he sped past her. To be sure, Walter was never late again. The very thought of being struck by his mother's big gold wedding ring put lightning in his feet.

Eighteen years have passed since Walter Kelly departed from this best of planets, but the memory of the beloved entertainer lives on, far from forgotten. Sincere tributes and appreciations of the man who gave so much of himself to vaudeville continue to appear occasionally in the columns. Wherever vaudeville is discussed, in the home, at the club, on Broadway, in all those places where oldtime show people gather to reminisce about "the good old days," the name Walter C. Kelly, alias "The Virginia Judge," inevitably pops up in the discussion.

It was a sad day for Walter when he began to sense that the golden age of vaudeville was passing. This was in the thirties, and Senator Ed Ford, later of radio's famed "Can You Top This?" program, remembers Walter's dire predictions of the days that were to come.

"Day by day I watch the gilded movie theatres, the improved programs of the 'small time' houses, and the radio slowly engulf the temple in which I have worshipped for a generation," Walter told a group of theatre goers one evening. "In the cycle of time it may bloom again, but I doubt it. The harsh demands of commerce, when applied to the theatre, seem to sound the death knell of whatever artistry it may lay claim to, and the class of vaudeville which once claimed Sarah Bernhardt, Cissie Loftus, Marie Dressler, Nat Wills, Will Mahoney, Elsie Janis and many others has passed on.

"From now on, fans of that kind of entertainment must be content with brown-derby saxophone players, noisy jazz bands, crooners of bedroom lyrics, and half-naked female dancing acts.

"All the romance and glamour of the stage have departed, because many of those who now control its future really belong in the field of commerce or industry."

Walter generally had a few million well-rounded words additionally to say, but you get the idea. He simply didn't like to stand by and watch what was happening to vaudeville —a slow death. But there wasn't much Walter or any of the other oldtime entertainers could do about the unhappy situation. Walter, as a matter of fact, spent his last several winters in the balmy tropics of Florida. His pals were largely from the sports world.

So well is he remembered as a star of vaudeville that folks are apt to forget that Walter also appeared in movies. His first role was in "Seas Beneath," a submarine picture starring George O'Brien.

Walter recalled that he had a "fair part," that of a chief gunner on a mystery ship named *Judy Ann.* John Ford directed the picture. At the outset, Walter was somewhat fearful. It was his belief that all directors assumed an air of I-am-the-Lord-thy-God, and were particularly hard on recruits from vaudeville. But Director Ford, with his warm sense of humor, was a refreshing switch from what Walter had anticipated, and everything went smoothly.

One of Walter's favorite stories about Hollywood involved a veteran acrobat who had a two-line role in a movie death scene. Dressed as a royal courtier, he was supposed to speak his two lines at the deathbed of the Prince of Ruritania. Panic suddenly seized him. The words wouldn't come.

"For God's sake," whispered the dying prince, "don't just stand there. Do something."

The old acrobat took his cue. Backing away from the couch, he did two perfect somersaults, bowed, and walked on out of the camera focus.

A gentleman of tremendous energy and genius, Walter spent many restless hours in those early years that separated him from obscurity and stardom. New York in those days was a "rubberneck paradise," and after rubbernecking at the many sights on Broadway, the Bowery, Greenwich Village, et al, he'd wander into the Astor Library, the Metropolitan Museum, the Aquarium, six-day bicycle races at the old Madison Square Garden, the theatres, boxing matches at the Coney Island Athletic Club and Maspeth, Long Island.

Walter ambled out of Tony Pastor's one night and went across to Sailor Tom Sharkey's bar. This was only a year after Sharkey had fought twenty-five rounds with Jim Jeffries, the heavyweight champion, and his star never shone brighter. Being a genuine fight fan, Walter asked to be introduced to Sailor Tom. This was done and, to properly impress Walter, Sharkey invited him upstairs to see his plush bachelor apartment. The fighter also asked Jabber Carey, a punch-drunk club fighter, to come along. Jabber was really gone. So many blows had he taken on the head that he was often seen talking to mail boxes. But Sailor Tom liked him and went out of his way to be kind to him.

Sharkey's boudoir was something to see. There were three

steel engravings of battleships and sailing vessels, more than a hundred photographs of pugs clipped from the *Police Gazette,* and directly over his bed, a painting of President Lincoln.

Sailor Tom reverently escorted his guests around the room, rattling off the records of the fighters and touching on the high moments of their greatest battles. Jabber's eye finally fell upon the portrait of Lincoln.

"Say, Tom," he asked, nonchalantly, "who'd the guy with the beard ever lick?"

The prize ring was one of Walter's biggest weaknesses. He loved the pugilists, saw most of the champions of his day in action, and he frequently arranged his tours so as to be on hand for a championship bout.

So it was in 1910, when Jim Jeffries came out of retirement to defend his world's heavyweight title against Jack Johnson, that Walter signed up for a coast-to-coast tour. He played his way through the Middle West, covered the South, went on to Texas, and was in Reno, Nevada, in time for the fight. There Walter met up with Jeffries and was invited to the champion's training camp.

"I always accompanied Jeff on his daily trout fishing expeditions or mountain hikes," related Walter later. "His wife asked me to do this because she wanted to get him away from the toil of fight talk of the general mob. On these trips the big fellow would get as playful as a Newfoundland pup and then, suddenly, would settle into a brooding silence. This worried me.

"I drove to San Francisco one afternoon with Tex Rickard, the promoter, to watch Johnson work out. He looked very good.

"A few days later I was back with Jeff again and on a hike in the mountains with him. We were walking along in silence, lost in our own thoughts, when Jeff suddenly spoke up.

" 'How does Johnson look?' he asked.

" 'Good,' I said. 'He looks ready to go.'

" 'He'd better be,' Jeff said. 'He may outbox me, but I'll show him up like I did Sharkey and Fitzsimmons.'

"That was the only time I ever heard him discuss the match.

"July Fourth arrived at last, bright and blistering. By noon the arena began to fill with spectators from every place imaginable. Old champions such as John L. Sullivan and Bob Fitzsimmons and Tom Sharkey and Stanley Ketchel were there.

"The fight? I will not try to describe it. It was the worst championship fight I ever saw. I walked across to Jeff's corner at the end of the fourth round and said to Jim Corbett, who had come out to advise and work out with the defending champion, 'Please, Jim, get him started. Give him a slug of brandy or something.'

"After Sam Berger, the referee, stepped in and stopped the slaughter of Jeff in the fifteenth round, the city of Reno emptied as quickly as it filled. It had been a terrible sight, the fall of a great champion. I remember bumping into Frank Gotch, world champion wrestler, and seeing the tears tumble down his cheeks. Me, I hid my grief at Lake Tahoe. We took our sports very seriously in those days."

Walter's despair over Jeff's defeat caused him to swear off all future prize fights, but his oath was short lived. He was booked to sail for Australia two months later, with stopovers in Honolulu and the Fiji Islands.

Aboard ship was Billy Papke, who was going to Australia to stage some exhibition bouts. Papke was former middleweight champion of the world. After stopping off for eighteen hours at Honolulu, the ship went on to the port of Suva. Since they were going to be in port for twenty-four hours, officers of the British Garrison at Suva arranged to stage some friendly bouts between several soldiers and some of the athletes aboard ship. The captain of the garrison asked Papke to fight his servant, Emmori. Emmori was a ferocious-looking native, six-foot tall and rugged. Papke weighed only 165, but agreed to the exhibition.

"Emmori is getting pretty chesty," the captain confided. "He learned a little boxing from some of the soldiers and thinks he can lick anybody. I want to teach him a lesson."

There were perhaps 300 natives in the crowd, every last one of them cheering for Emmori. Walter was the timekeeper. Amid savage cries, Emmori tore into Papke at the sound of the opening bell. He was swinging like a windmill. The air was filled with flailing leather. Not one landed on Papke's jaw, as he feinted, parried and dodged the shots expertly.

While the fighters rested between rounds, Walter walked over to Papke's corner and whispered, "You'd better hurry and knock out this cannibal, or he may bite you."

Billy said nothing, only nodded.

Walter whomped the bell again and Emmori charged the ex-champion on a dead run. Papke cleverly sidestepped Emmori and jolted him with a left uppercut. Emmori, with the shrieks of his fellow natives rising in a crescendo behind him, halted his advance, a furious and stunned expression spread across his face. Before he could recover his senses, Papke hit him again, flush on the jaw. Emmori dropped like he'd been slugged by a triphammer. There he lay, not moving a muscle.

Instantly the three hundred natives began chorusing the strangest and most spine-tingling song Walter ever had heard. He later learned that it was their Death Song. Emmori was dead, they were certain. But Emmori fortunately was revived minutes later and the Death Song stopped.

While in Sydney, Australia, to keep an engagement at the Tivoli, Walter met and enjoyed the company of who was perhaps the cleverest boxer of all time—Albert Griffith, alias Young Griffo. Oddly enough, this colorful character from Sydney contributed nothing to the sport except his incredible ability which defied description. He fought anyone from featherweights to middleweights. Young Griffo's favorite prank was to walk up to a bootblack's stand, remove his shoes, and have his feet shined.

Griff was standing at a bar in a saloon one night when in walked a fellow who had been going around town telling everyone what he was going to do to the professional fighter if ever they met face to face.

The bartender turned to Griffo and said, "Here he is now, Griff, that guy who has been looking for you so he can punch you in the nose."

Griffo didn't turn around. He merely stared at the large mirror behind the bar. The intruder came over and began swinging at Griffo's head. Griff blandly watched the attack in the mirror, ducking and dodging the blows accordingly. Finally, exhausted from fanning the air, the fellow grabbed Griffo by the shoulders, spun him around, and cried:

"Okay, Griffo, you win. I was gonna knock your block off, but ya' ain't got one. I'm licked without being struck."

"Griffo used to employ his dazzling speed to win barroom wagers or, when his finances were low, drinks," Walter Kelly told Harry Grayson, the veteran sports editor, one time. "One of his favorite tricks was to enter a saloon, spread a small handkerchief on the floor, step on it, then challenge anyone in the house to hit him while he held both hands behind his back and remained rooted within the small area of the nose wiper. No one ever succeeded in laying a hand on him as he twisted and ducked away from the punches without moving his feet.

"But his greatest demonstration of speed was flycatching. He would swoop a fly from the bar, release it in the air, then catch it again in the air, between his thumb and index finger!

"I remember the time that Griff came to this country and was matched for a bout in Springfield, Illinois," continued Walter, giving his listener a Grade-A history lesson on pugilism. "His manager tried desperately to make him train. No luck. Psychology was finally applied.

" 'Griff,' the manager warned, 'you're gonna meet a man-eater this time. We've been duped. I would not have matched you with this guy if I had known he was so tough.'

"Griffo cocked his ears. He was obviously impressed, if not astonished.

" 'A man-eater, says yer?' he replied in his best cockney. 'Blime me, ol' chappie, who ez'e? The devil with 'im. I'll knock 'im silly, I will!'

"The manager saw it was working and he decided to go further.

" 'You know, Griff, this guy you're fighting went 198 rounds with a feller and he could have gone another hundred. You gotta nail him early or he will keep you fighting all night.'

"Griffo appeared definitely worried now, though the truth was that his next opponent was nothing but a bum.

" 'He went 198 rounds, did 'e?' snarled Griffo. 'A man-eater, eh?' So he quit drinking and trained harder than ever. He was in first-class condition by the time of the fight.

"At the opening bell he sailed into his opponent like a hungry bulldog jumping on a tenderloin steak. He had the poor fellow draped on the ring ropes, bloody and startled, when the riot squad was rushed in to stop the fight.

" 'Zowie! What a beating you gave him,' cried his manager in the dressing room.

" 'Beat 'im up?' Griffo said. 'I should rawther say so. I took no chance of that bleedin' duck goin' 198 rounds with me.'

"Later, when Griffo learned the truth, he tore into a rage.

" 'Just think of it,' he roared, 'me givin' up me drink to train for a raw 'un. The pleasure I gave up and the fun I lost trainin' for the loikes o' 'im!' "

George Ade, who was one of Walter's closest friends in the world of the theatre, once said that if he had to give a capsule description of the "Judge," he would do it thusly:

"A wise and extraordinary man. A placid philosopher, and an impromptu speaker of uncommon merit. A lover of quaint characters. A man among men, superbly masculine, and quite unspoiled. Certainly a wonderful ornament to his generation."

Author Ade said that he was always the enthralled listener in Walter's presence. "He was a humorist of the first water," testified Ade, "and one of the men I have put into my private Hall of Fame. I had a deep affection and respect for him, for his attitude toward me was that of a tolerant and sympathetic father."

No matter where Walter traveled, nor the nature of the gathering, folks were constantly urging him to tell stories in that gruff, slightly hard-boiled style of his.

"He was one of the funniest men I ever met," said Harry Grayson. "Walter entertained at many a sports dinner and always was a hit. Because of his intimate acquaintance with champions of all sorts, he was right at home with the sports crowd.

"But the best of all Walter's stories—and he was always asked to repeat it—was the Irish story about the parish priest meeting Mary O'Toole one day on the street. Mary wore a cape which concealed something under her arm. Highly familiar with Mary's weakness for hard drink, the priest inquired, 'Mary, what on earth are you packing under your cape?'

"Hopefully, Mary replied, 'Holy water, Father.'

" 'Let me see,' commanded the priest, taking the cork out of the bottle and smelling it. 'This is not holy water. It's whiskey.'

"'Glory be to God,' cried Mary, crossing herself, 'another miracle!'"

What manner of young man was Walter Kelly when he was growing up back in East Falls, Pennsylvania? Well, he was this kind of boy, brimful of life and vigor:

Walter was sitting in the local East Falls literary club one day, absently staring out the window, when he spotted Hughie Murphy, the town huckster and drunk, stumbling into a bar across the street. A little white light flashed on in Walter's head. He knew that Murphy would be occupied at the bar indefinitely.

Walter sprang from his chair like he'd been stuck by a fork, bolted out the door and across the street, and grabbed Murphy's horses parked outside the pub. He took them and hid them up the street behind a shed. Then he ran back to the saloon.

"Murphy! . . . Murphy!" he shrieked, "somebody's stolen your horses! Com'on, let's go find 'em."

Murphy stumbled out the door, saw his horses gone, and marched off to fetch the police.

"My horses," he cried to the police, "they've been swiped. You gotta help me ketch the blighters."

While the desperate Murphy was off fetching the law, Walter returned to the shed and sneaked the horses back to their original parking place. When the police arrived to investigate—lo and behold, there were Murphy's horses, as peaceful as you please. The policemen glared at Murphy with tolerant understanding.

"Murphy," they said, "you're drunk again. Do us a favor, will ya'? Lay off that cheap booze and try the dollar stuff for a change."

Walter stood back and chuckled.

Walter had just turned twenty when he got the itch to

travel and go out on his own. He had spent four years as an apprentice machinist at the Baldwin Locomotive and Midvale Steel Works in Philadelphia, and he had heard they were looking for machinists down at the Newport News, Virginia, shipyards. After much persuasion, he finally talked his parents into letting him go. So, equipped only with a cheap little suitcase, boundless optimism, and love of adventure, Walter left home.

It was a blustery, cold March morning when Walter arrived at Old Point Comfort, Virginia, on his way to Newport News. A dusty ride in a one-track trolley through Hampton and Phoebus, followed by several miles of vacant, flat, scrub pinelands, finally set him down in Newport News.

Little did Walter imagine that in this sleepy and drowsy town he would find the key to a future life of pleasure and profit beyond his wildest dreams.

Walter lost no time getting a job at the Huntington Shipyards. He worked steadily until the Spanish-American War broke out, then enlisted as a machinist mate on a troop-carrying steamship named *Grand Duchess*. To add to his income, the enterprising Walter also opened a canteen on board. By the time the shooting stopped, he had a bankroll of more than $2500.

Walter returned from the war with his pockets bulging with gold and silver. There was a lively little establishment in Newport News named the Mecca Cafe, and Walter bought it. Business flourished for the first three months and Walter began to send messages home telling the family that they could all soon retire. Walter would take care of them. This optimism was short lived, however, owing to an ingenious credit system Walter had extended to shipyard cronies and an increasing aloofness between his bartenders and the cash register.

But those were gay days and nights at the Mecca Cafe notwithstanding. A frowsy old bum walked in one afternoon and tapped Walter on the shoulder.

"Mister," said the panhandler, "can you spare a quarter for a drink for an incorrigible old bum?"

Walter stared at the man in utter amusement. He was so delighted by the bum's honesty and the fact that he pronounced incorrigible with a hard g, that he gave him a five dollar bill and sent him happily on his way. Walter was a soft touch.

Shortly after the Mecca's grand opening, a smooth, polished-looking fellow came in to see Walter. He said he was from Kansas City, and he was carrying a fat bank roll.

"I'd like to rent the second floor above your place," the stranger said.

"What for?" inquired Walter. "Plan to settle down and live here?"

"I'm not thinking of living up there," the man said. "I want to open a *palais de chance.*"

"A what?" asked Walter.

"Gaming room," the man explained.

Walter did some fast calculating. Maybe it would be good for business. Even gambling people had to eat.

"All right," Walter said. "I will rent you the space."

Soon the second floor above Walter's cafe was noisy with eager beavers trying to beat roulette, chuck-a-luck and bird cage, faro bank, and a keno layout. Everything was running perfectly until a local preacher heard about it. By gum, gambling was a sin, he howled. This called for action. A demon for publicity, he launched an anti-gambling crusade and even got the town's newspaper lauding his fiery campaign.

At first Walter paid no heed to the attack. It would blow over. But it didn't blow over. If anything, it got worse. Walter glanced out of his cafe one night and there was the minister, on his knees in front of a platoon of gospel singers, praying to save both Walter and the town from the eternal fires of Hell.

Walter got ahold of his Kansas City tenant for a meeting of the minds.

"This is bad for business," Walter said.

"Yes," the Jayhawker agreed. "We've got to get that bird off his knees and off our backs."

Walter rubbed his chin contemplatively, figuring out a counter-attack. He recollected that the Salvation Army was in town and needed space for a headquarters. They had no funds.

"What do you say we let them use the third floor of our building, rent free," Walter said. "I will also put in chairs and a platform."

Splendid suggestion, the Kansan replied.

Walter went to the director of the Salvation Army and told of the plan. The Salvationist was so grateful he showered Walter with blessings. The SA leader made immediate arrangements for a huge opening the following Saturday night.

Local natives had never seen anything quite like it before. Twice weekly, on the same evenings, the preacher and his disciples knelt outside the Mecca and called on God to show Walter the way of righteousness, while up through the gaming rooms passed the Salvationists to their temple on the third floor, asking the Lord to send His choicest blessings on Walter's head.

It put the Lord in an embarrassing position.

The roulette wheel clicked on the second floor, and on the ground level drunken sailors cavorted. Bottles flew, beer suds sailed over the bar, and life rolled merrily on.

During his several years at Newport News, Walter became inoculated with the political virus that courses through the veins of every person south of Baltimore. Somebody anonymously put Walter's name on the ballot in the district's Congressional race, and Walter started out, with horse and buggy, to make the South forget William Jennings Bryan's "Crown of Thorns" and "Cross of Gold" orations.

How Virginia rocked to Walter's campaigning. Caesar, Alexander and Napoleon were nonentities by comparison. Walter ranted on and on. His speeches sounded so convincing that he began to believe them himself. How could he lose! As a show of confidence, he wagered his cafe on the election. Later, Walter was to wonder why God, in His infinite wisdom and pity, did not save youth from such foolhardiness.

The election results? Walter lost—by one vote!—and with it his establishment.

With the laments of political defeat taunting him, Walter, fortified by the wisdom of experience, went back to the more practical but less romantic occupation of installing engines in steamboats.

Laid off temporarily, Walter wandered aimlessly into the Newport News police court one sultry evening to watch his old fishing companion, Judge John Dudley Brown, dispose of petty offenders, most of whom were Negroes. Judge Brown was a tall, gaunt, serious-looking Virginian, with a quaint but richly warm nature. He courted a broad philosophy, whimsical humor, and a devout love of justice.

Pinpointed, that maiden visit to Judge Brown's crude Temple of Justice must be credited with bringing the most important change in Walter Kelly's professional life. The transformation began with the appearance of the very first Negro prisoner Judge Brown called to the bar.

Staring down at a lean, stoop-shouldered defendant, Judge Brown observed, "Jim Williams, you are charged with feloniously cutting and wounding the body and person of Lindsey Gault. What have you to say?"

"Jedge, I wants to plead not guilty," said Jim Williams. "I

didn't want to cut nobody. I jes' sorta pushed dat li'l ol' knife to'd him and it seem lak he run right into it."

Judge Brown fought back a twinkle of a smile.

"Jim" he continued, "this is a serious case. Have you a lawyer?"

"No, suh, I don't want no lawyer messin' around me. Dey costs a-plenty. But if you don't mind, Jedge, I sure 'nuff would lak a couple good witnesses."

"Jim, just what do you propose to do for a defense since you have no lawyer?"

"Jedge, if you don't mind, I would jes' as leave let the whole thing drop."

"Well, Jim, this is the third time you have been up here for cutting folks. How old are you?"

"I'se jes' twenty-fo', Jedge."

Without changing his expression, Judge Brown said, "Well, Jim, you will be just twenty-five when you get out. Next case."

A vagrant Negro was ushered before the bar. Judge Brown appraised him carefully before speaking.

"Mose," he said, "what are you doing back here in town again after I told you to go on home?"

Mose shifted nervously from one foot to the other as if his feet itched.

"I wuz jes' circulatin', Jedge."

Judge Brown waved to his jailor.

"Dan," he ordered, "take this edition out of circulation for thirty days."

In the days that followed, the local police court became Walter's regular haunt. It was a familiar sight to see him sitting in the back and jotting down notes of the hilarious repartee.

So that this heretofore untapped and untold comedy and pathos would be preserved for mankind, Walter originated a series of monologues.

On his last visit to the court room, Walter picked up this jewel for his act:

Henry Harper was pushed before Judge Brown. The old Negro smelled of cheap whiskey and teetered on legs as unsteady as a new-born colt's.

"Drunk again, eh, Henry?" the judge said. "You have been arrested five times in the past six weeks."

Ol' Henry looked at His Honor apologetically.

"Yazzuh, Jedge," he said, "I woulda been here dat other week, too, but I'se got arrested over at Phoebus and couldn't come."

And so, armed with a simple portrayal in dialect of the jocularity he witnessed in Judge Brown's court, Walter said goodby to Virginia and departed for Broadway. Gone were the worries about how he would make his fortune.

Swinging breezily down the Great White Way with his little paper suitcase and twenty-five dollars, Walter Kelly dreamt rosy dreams which soon were to come true.

A Star Is Born

In his first engagement in New York, Walter became a smash hit practically overnight, and the rush was on to bill him at all the leading show palaces throughout the country. Walter decided to sign up with the old Keith Circuit, but before going on the road he ran down to East Falls to see the family for the first time since crashing the big time.

He arrived home all dolled up in a gray-checkered suit, bright yellow-russet shoes, white socks, a vibrant-hued coat, and a two-dollar sailor straw skimmer with a red and blue ribbon band. For an extra touch, he carried a walking stick. He was very proud of himself.

"Hey, Ma!" he shouted, opening the front door, "I'm home!" He put down his suitcase and waited for his mother to come downstairs.

"Walter!" cried Mary Kelly, spotting her son. "Let me look at you."

Walter did a spin in the middle of the room.

"Well, Ma, how do you like the suit?" he asked. "The best money can buy, Ma. Real class, huh?"

Mary Kelly eyed her son with affection, then tolerant understanding. Before she could speak, her husband and Grandfather Costello, who was visiting the family, walked into the room. Walter greeted them loudly, then said, "What do you think of your son now, dad?"

John Kelly, who had never been in a theatre in his life, scowled at his boy's attire. He was speechless. The Kellys lived right behind St. Bridget's Church, and after seventy-five-year-old Grandfather Costello had sized his grandson up and down, he said with a rich brogue, "Holy Killarney! Stay inside, lad—don't let the priest see ya'!"

At dinner that evening, Walter was the center of attention. He was the first of the Kellys to make a name in the theatre, and his family wanted him to know they were proud of him. Elizabeth and Grace stared at Walter in blank admiration. Jack and George beamed at him. Noting the wondering gaze of his two younger brothers, little did Walter suspect that there would come a day when both would achieve fame and fortune, too.

Mother Kelly rapped for silence.

"Shhh," she hushed. "Give Walter a chance to talk."

The others wanted to hear details about the night Walter substituted for the incomparable Marie Dressler. He had been signed with the great lady of the stage in a musical production. When the show opened on Broadway, Miss Dressler was suddenly bedded by an acute attack of laryngitis. Word of her plight was slow reaching the theatre management. Fifteen minutes before curtain time the news arrived, throwing Producer Percy Williams into a panic.

Percy suddenly recalled hearing Walter do an act at the Green Room Club in New York some months before. The Green Room was the place where for the first time Walter had given his impersonation of the character he later made world-famous, The Virginia Judge.

Producer Williams grabbed Walter and said, "You're going out there in place of Marie tonight. Do anything, but entertain them."

Frank Girard, the stage manager, walked out and explained to the audience that Marie was sick and couldn't perform. He offered to refund the ticket money to those who wished it. Then he told them that Walter Kelly would do a novelty act. Some of the customers left, but others came in and took their places. Walter borrowed Girard's judicial-looking Prince Albert and, with a chair leg for a gavel, went into his act.

Rapping the gavel, Walter shouted, "I want order in the court. Dan, get those dogs away from that stove. It smells like a tan yard in here. First case on the docket—Sadie Anderson.

" 'Yes, sir, that's me.'

"Thirty days in jail, that's me.

"Next case—Rufus Johnson. Rufus, you're charged with larceny of two chickens from the premises of Howard Brooks on Brierfield Road. What have you to say for yourself?

" 'Wal, Jedge, I never was near Mr. Brooks' house and the Lord may strike me dead if I stole those chickens.'

"Rufus, you stand aside for ten minutes, and if the Lord don't strike you, I will give you thirty days."

That was the beginning of the Virginia Judge, one of the all-time great vaudeville acts. Walter took so many encores the first night that Percy Williams told him his future on the stage definitely had to be as a solo. Marie Dressler retired to a rest camp and Walter finished the engagement alone with star billing.

Now he was receiving $1000 a week, and Grandfather Costello, who hadn't been inside a theatre in decades, said he figured that his grandson either had to be a porch-climbing house burglar or a first-rate bank robber to command all that money.

"What tools are you using, lad?" Grandfather Costello asked.

"Tools?" said Walter, puzzled.

"I mean," Grandfather Costello said, "what other work do you do beside all that gab to be gettin' all that money?"

"That's all," said Walter, "that's all I have to do."

"Begorra!" snapped Grandfather Costello, "the people can't all be crazy, lad, so get it while the gettin's good."

That evening, as the Kellys sat around the table enjoying Walter's company for the first time in a couple of years, they celebrated the occasion by serving steak. Grandfather Costello, who'd had his belly full of genteel poverty and could not forget the threadbare years as a boy in Ireland during the potato blight, grew silent as a fat porterhouse steak was placed in front of him.

Jack caught the look on his granddad's face, and inquired, "Something wrong, Granddad?"

"The world's upside down," muttered Granddad Costello. "For years I had good teeth and nothing to eat in Ireland. Now here I am with a steak big enough to wrap a child in, and not a dolgone tooth left!"

Walter stayed home for a few days, then left to do a midweek matinee in Pittsburgh. He was following Clayton, White and Marie Stuart, renowned sketch artists of the day, when in the middle of his performance a raging fire broke out in the building next to the theatre. Balloons of smoke billowed around him. The customers rushed for the exits. Walter stopped his monologue and assumed his most nonchalant manner.

The whole story of the Kelly family is a remarkable one, but the supreme figure in it was mother Mary Kelly.

John Henry Kelly, a handsome man, came to the United States from Ireland when he was twenty; started as an unskilled laborer and went on to build a flourishing insurance business.

Walter Kelly, the beloved "Virginia Judge" of vaudeville, became internationally famous.

George Kelly had his heart set on the theater since childhood, went on to win acclaim as a Pulitzer Prize playwright.

Jack Kelly, center, with his cap off, had to learn a trade, and he chose brick laying. He began by working for his brother P. H.'s construction company.

The "Virginia Judge," Walter C. Kelly.

Despite his father's objections, Jack Kelly also played football. He was good enough to receive a few college offers.

World's singles sculls champion in 1920, Jack Kelly has been voted greatest oarsman in U. S. history. He once won 126 races in 1919 and 1920.

Jack teamed with cousin, Paul Costello, to win 1920 and 1924 Olympic Games double sculls. In all the years they rowed together, they never lost a race.

The "Judge," Walter Kelly, conducts a Kangaroo Court at Jim Jeffries' training camp in 1910, all part of the fun.

Walter Kelly visits the courtroom of Judge John Dudley Brown, pictured on his left. It was here that the "Virginia Judge" originated his famous vaudeville monologue.

World's champions: Kelly, Man o' War, and Jack Dempsey.

Kelly For Brickwork. This is the way his headquarters looked in the 1930's. Today John B. Kelly, Inc., has grown into the biggest masonry company in the country.

Jack Kelly, standing on right with arms folded, poses with some of his World War I Army buddies. Jack enlisted as a private, was commissioned on the battle field.

Jack Kelly still knows how to lay a brick or two. This photo was taken at his Summer place in 1956.

A star among Hollywood stars. Handsome Jack was invited to the cinema city to test for a movie role years ago, but the plans never materialized. That's Henry Fonda on his left, George Brent and Henry O'Neil on his right.

Jim Farley, center, and Jack Kelly worked in close harmony for the National Democratic Party in the 1930's.

A baseball fan extraordinary, Kelly chats with Jimmy Foxx, the Athletics' home run hero two decades ago. Jack almost bought the Philadelphia Phillies at one time.

Vote for Kelly, Jack told Philadelphia voters. He barely lost election in 1935 mayoralty race.

Drafted into politics, Jack got out and campaigned for votes among all groups.

"That's my Pop," says Peggy Kelly, pointing to picture of her father during 1935 mayoralty race. That's Grace Kelly on left, Kell on right.

Mr. and Mrs. John B. Kelly cast their ballots during the tight '35 election. Jack polled more votes than any previous Democratic candidate.

Kell developed strong muscles as a youngster frolicking on the beach at Ocean City, New Jersey.

The beginning. Kell began the long, arduous pull toward the coveted Diamond Sculls championship at the age of seven.

Kell was the apple of his parents' eyes.

Brother, sister and father Kelly prepare rowboat for workout.

"Ladies and gents," he announced, "owing to a slight blaze next door, we will temporarily dismiss you."

And then, nodding to the orchestra leader, he said, "Ted, my exit number please."

Standing on the stage with a forced smile, in clouds of swirling smoke, Walter Kelly watched the audience depart—fast.

Those were unpredictable, glorious days for Walter. The conditions under which he performed were not always the best. One of his stops was Atlantic City. The vaudeville house had no dressing room, except for a space of about eight feet, between the backdrop and wall running parallel across the stage, and, as a gesture of privacy for the ladies and men of the traveling vaudeville groups, divided by a horribly-soiled cretonne curtain. A poorly painted and tarnished backdrop constituted the lone barrier between dressing rooms and audience.

One of the acts in Walter's troupe was Bisguin & Snogay, statue clog dancers. They worked on marble slabs under an amber spotlight. Their costumes consisted of skin tight white tights and shirt, white wool wigs and clogs. Their faces were chalked.

They had just completed their act and, owing to the heat, they retired to their dressing quarters to strip off their costumes and make-up. There they stood, completely naked, backs to the audience over washstands, when a drunken stage hand was ordered to pull up a border. A Japanese troupe of acrobats were following the hoofers and they needed more room for their act. By mistake, the drunk grasped the backdrop line—and, alas, there to the amazement of the startled audience, stood the undraped Bisguin & Snogay.

Bisguin, his eyes filled with soap, and totally unconscious of the roar of the crowd, turned to his partner.

"Geez, Snogay," he said, "they're sure fallin' for those Japs, ain't they!"

After Atlantic City came Buffalo, New York, and Walter was billed to precede a famous trained dog act, composed of greyhounds, poodles and terriers. The dogs waited patiently backstage as Walter wound up his monologue. There were sixteen of them in the act, and the lady dogs wore fancy dresses, panties and gay bonnets, the males were attired in bright colored trousers and high hats. Two were dressed as clowns. They were lined up on fancy painted little pedestals as they waited for Walter to finish.

Just before Walter's exit, a mangy, belligerent-looking black cat strolled through the back door of the theatre from the alley. Unseen by the dog trainer, Mr. Tomcat walked in full view of the pooches.

Instantly the air was full of barking dogs. The most surprised and scared tomcat ever to crash a theatre made for the door in two leaps. Out the door in full pursuit and down the alley bolted the dog act—the greyhounds with high hats askew, terriers losing their trousers, and the lady dogs tripping over their dignity.

"Due to unforeseen circumstances," announced the embarrassed theatre manager moments later, "the Meehan dog act will not appear tonight."

Hours later the dog trainer, his arms full of doggie lingerie, was still exploring the back alleys of Buffalo searching for the sixteen most expensive animals in town.

That was one cat that never came back.

Walter played in some mighty tough towns. Every hotel clerk was named Jesse James. "How much for a room?" Walter would inquire. And the clerk's stock reply was, "How much have you got? That's what it costs and it has to be paid in advance."

Along the way Walter appeared with Will Rogers on the

same bill at Hammerstein's. Rogers had just closed with a Wild West outfit, and he was tackling vaudeville for the first time. He rode a horse on stage, yelling like a Pawnee with a hotfoot, carrying a lariat and chomping away on a mouthful of gum. Walter stood in the wings with Willie Hammerstein, and he said, "That fella's going to be a star in this business." And Willie said, "You're right, but why on earth does he need that horse and the chewing gum?"

Rogers was a smash hit, and on closing night Walter asked the little Negro groom, who cared for Will's horse, where his boss was playing the following week. The Negro groom looked at Walter glumly.

"I don't know, suh," he replied, "I'se quittin' tonight."

Walter asked him why.

"I'se sorta likes Mr. Rogers," he said, "but I grieves to tell you dat he bin payin' fo' dollahs for my hotel room, an' de las' couple nights he bin sorta hintin' I'se oughta give up de room and sleep wid his horse. I'se agin dat!"

Walter's swing on the old Keith Circuit that year included engagements in Washington, Atlanta, Baltimore and Philadelphia. He was leaving the Forsythe Theatre in Atlanta one afternoon when he saw an old colored gent sunning himself against the building across from the stage entrance. Walter was lugging a suitcase that weighed a ton. He struggled over to the old man.

"D'ya want to make a quarter, Dad?" he asked.

The old man eyed the suitcase skeptically.

"No, suh," he drawled, "Ah's already got a quarter."

Walter also played the old Keith House at Portland, Maine. He later admitted it was the toughest town he ever performed in. Portland had a typical one-night stand op'ry house, clean but with no ventilation backstage. The stage lighting system was poor, and the audience reminded Walter of a coroner's jury. Performers called it "The Morgue." But the stage manager had a warm sense of humor, and that took some of the curse off of it. He kept a large ledger backstage, and on closing night he always asked the performers to write their opinions of the place. This is what Walter's good friend, W. C. Fields, put down:

"W. C. Fields; born Philadelphia, 1874. Died at every performance, Portland, Maine, 1907."

Walter became such a huge success in the United States that he began to get offers from abroad. He agreed to appear at the Palace Theatre in London at a hundred pounds a week. Shortly before his boat sailed he returned home again.

At a family dinner, Grandfather Costello, whose early years in Ireland had been dedicated to a ceaseless guerilla warfare against English landlords, solemnly advised his grandson to cancel the Palace engagement.

"The mere mention of the name Kelly will destroy any chance of success," the old man said.

Walter arrived in London a week before his big opening. One of the first things he did was to take a stroll from the Hotel Cecil, where he was lodging, along the Strand down toward Trafalgar Square. He wanted to get a *feel* of the city. Along the way he saw a sign on a double-deck bus which announced in huge bold, black letters: "Exclusive Engagement At The Palace, Direct From America—Walter C. Kelly, The Virginia Judge."

Walter was filled with alarm. Supposing, after so stellar a notice, he couldn't live up to the advance fanfare. Perhaps his southern act wouldn't be understood in London. Already he could hear the heckleberries, loud and clear.

Walter returned to his hotel room. First he edited his material, then rushed out and caught the English comedians at the Tivoli, Oxford, Pavillion and Empire. He spent the rest of the night overhauling his act to conform with British tastes.

Came the opening night and Walter was frightened. Minutes before his stage call, he sent a boy out to get a pint of champagne to sooth his rattled nerves. It buoyed him up considerably. When the rap at his dressing room door came —"You're on next, Mr. Kelly"—the nervousness was almost gone. With a prayer to a thousand Irish ancestors, Walter cried, "Kelly against England—charge!"

To make a short story shorter, since it was customary for the serenely proper Palace audience not to applaud a stranger, Walter walked onto the stage in absolute silence. Was this going to be one of those most bitter of all disappointments to an American actor, a London flop?

Walter's first recollection, after reaching the center of the stage, was the sound of far-away laughter, followed by his seeming emergence from some great depth, then another louder and heart-warming burst of chuckling, and with it the assurance that all was going to be well.

At the accompaniment of the orchestra playing "I Was Born In Virginia," Walter quickly decided to stick to his regular Virginia Judge routine and in five minutes had the Londoners in thc palm of his hand. He glanced offstage, and there stood the normally stolid and reserved Alfred Butt, the Palace manager, beaming with pleasure. Walter disappeared into the wings twenty minutes later, floating on fluffy clouds, ready to become a British subject. All his worry and fretting had been needless.

The critics raved about "The Virginia Judge" in the papers the following morning. Agents streamed into his hotel room with handsome offers to do his bit in all the major European cities. His Majesty the King requested a private performance. The Palace management wanted to extend its original four weeks' contract.

Walter agreed to play another four weeks at the Palace, and eight weeks annually for the next four years. He wound up his Palace engagement early in August, with a farewell curtain speech to a rousing ovation he never forgot.

Walter's merry travels took him next to Scotland, and an opening at the Pavillion in Glasgow. It rained daily during his first week there. Walter thought perhaps he had his seasons mixed. Collaring the old stage doorman at the Pavillion, Walter asked, "Just when do you have summer up here?"

"I dinna know exactly," the old gentleman said, scratching his chin reflectively, "but I think it was on a Wednesday last year."

In Dublin, Walter played golf with the manager of the theatre where he was starring. Walter was not much of a golfer. He said he would do much better with a shovel than a niblick. Caddies were scarce and Walter and his friend had to carry their own clubs. At the fourth green Walter spotted an Irish lad leaning over the fence watching him three-putt the hole. Walter stopped and called to the boy.

"Son, how'd you like to caddy for me?" he asked.

"How do you caddy?" the boy replied.

"All you have to do is carry these clubs and watch the ball for me," explained Walter.

"Sure," responded the boy.

The youngster seemed pleased with the job. When Walter gave him four shillings his eyes bugged out like hard-boiled eggs.

Walter asked, "Is that enough?"

"It's twice as much as I expected," the boy said. He paused.

"Something wrong, son?" Walter asked.

"I was just wondering, sir," the boy said, "will you be out *diggin'* this way again tomorrow?"

While appearing at the Gaiety in Dublin, Walter was visited backstage one night by a priest.

"Mr. Kelly," the priest said, "I wonder if you will do me a favor—a big favor."

"Of course, Father."

"Well," said the priest, "my parish is sponsoring a concert to raise money and it would help a lot if you came and entertained."

"I'd be happy to, Father."

The parish was located forty miles outside Dublin, and Walter rode the distance in an open hackney coach. Rain was pouring and Walter arrived soaking wet. But rather than keep the parishioners waiting, he insisted upon going into his act immediately. The parish was crowded to overflowing. Walter thrilled the audience with an Irish routine for two hours.

Later, he asked the priest, "What about the receipts, Father?"

"We collected twenty pounds, more than we've ever taken in," the priest said.

"Sshhh," Walter said, "we've got to keep this quiet. If that figure gets out, program managers all over the world will cancel my act."

The priest was plainly embarrassed. He had intended to boast about the receipts to the bishop.

"I'll tell you what, Father," said Walter. "I don't think it would be too bad if you said you took in forty pounds." And pulling out his wallet, he thrust another twenty pounds into the priest's hand. "Good night, Father," he said, winking broadly. "Thanks for the wonderful time your parishioners showed me."

And watching him swing merrily out the door, the priest thought, "There he goes, off into the dark night, before I can offer that grand, generous man a wee dram or even a bit of food."

Athletically, Walter was a fine swimmer. He won the James River Mile Championship while living in Newport News, Virginia, but he often chided himself by saying that the Lord never designed him for any other form of exercise. "But He did give me a strong voice to cheer the other boys on to win," added Walter.

Walter found plenty to cheer about during his London engagement in 1908, the year the Olympic Games were staged in England.

On the afternoon of the Olympic Marathon, Walter was the boxseat guest of Sir Thomas Lipton and Lord Dewar. They sat not more than twenty feet from the royal box. Shepards Bush Stadium was packed with 90,000 spectators, two-thirds of them Britishers. There were perhaps 4000 Americans, mostly college boys from our universities.

The marathoners started from Windsor Castle. Great Britain entered twelve runners. Nobody had heard of Johnny Hayes, America's star candidate.

After a spell, the loud speaker announcer finally shouted that the contestants were nearing the stadium.

"Dorando, of Italy, is leading . . . Mike Heffernan, of South Africa, is second . . ."

No mention was made of Johnny Hayes.

The Italian staggered in under the stadium ramp. He still had another 385 yards to go. Sixty yards later he collapsed. Suddenly, as if out of thin air, a smallish fellow came trotting along the ramp like a coach dog. Who was he? Two Britishers back of Walter focused their binoculars.

"I cawn't recognize him," said one. " 'Ere, 'arry, you take the glasses."

'arry peered a moment and then smote his forehead.

"God's truth, it's a Yank!" he exclaimed.

This was Walter's cue and he began to cheer. One of the Englishmen behind Walter fetched him a whack over the head with his binoculars.

"Sit down, you bloody Yank!" he roared.

"Sit down yourself, you so-and-so!" retorted Walter.

"Where are your Englishmen? They ought to be up front. George Washington taught you Britishers how to run!"

The Englishman sat down.

Italian confederates ran onto the track and surrounded Dorando. They got him back up on his feet and he ran another 100 yards before collapsing again. By now the identity of Hayes had been discovered.

"It's 'eys," cried the Britishers around Walter.

The Italians carried Dorando across the finish line, automatically disqualifying him. Hayes came dogtrotting behind him, trailed by Heffernan and another American, Forshaw, of St. Louis. Hayes, declared the winner, of course, walked off the track with 60,000 Britishers booing him. But as he passed the American section, "It's A Grand Old Flag" was being sung by the U.S. college boys and could be heard above the roar of the mob. Walter felt proud of his country.

England, to put it baldly, was one vast cemetery that night. On the way home from the stadium, Walter, masquerading behind an English accent, asked a newsboy who had won the marathon.

"I 'ates to tell you, sir," the newsboy said, "but it was a bleddy Yenkee by the name o' Hyes."

What a victory! What a night! What a time!

Dorando was reported dying in a hospital from exhaustion. Walter was reported cleaning up English waiters at the Savoy. Walter had three pretty fair bodyguards with him—Ralph Rose, a huge shot-putter, and Kid McCoy and Jimmy Britt, champion fist-fighters.

They were arrested three times that night.

One Man In A Boat

When the air is soft and fleeting
And the Schuylkill still at night
There glides a silent oarsman
Who rides with silent might.

And fast and swift the shell glides
Through years and tender dreams
And they say his name is Kelly
And he's master of the streams.
—by Dave Stidolph

While Walter was well on his way to becoming an international headliner in show business, back in East Falls brother Jack was developing into a strapping, handsome young man of six-foot-two, 175 pounds, with the animal strength of a Sampson.

Rowing, by now, had become a momentous, serious, day-to-day battle to which Jack was supplying all of his emotion and energy. While his pals played, Jack was out on the river tugging away on the work end of his oars. As much as he enjoyed a good time, there was no time for play, because he wanted to be a champion some day. His normal schedule called for getting up each morning at six, sometimes earlier, be on his bricklaying job at seven, work until five, then rush over to Boathouse Row and pull away on the oars until nightfall.

Jack was usually in bed at ten o'clock. Occasionally he dropped into the neighborhood ice cream parlor, where some of his chums hung out, downed a quart of ice cream while barbering with the boys, then turned in. He went for that ice cream a mile a minute. On Sundays he attended early Mass, and spent the rest of the day rowing.

His mother began to view his rigid training program with marked alarm. It worried her.

"You're killing yourself, boy," she said one night, sitting alone with Jack in the kitchen as she watched him eat supper. Jack always ate late because he was out on the river when the rest of the family had dinner. His mother kept a plate of food warming for him in the oven. "Why do you punish yourself so? Is rowing that important to you?"

"Ma," Jack said, "I want to be the national champion some day. And I'm a long way from that yet."

"But why rowing?" she said. "Why don't you concentrate on baseball, or football, or basketball? You're good at them all."

Jack grew silent, then managed a faint smile, and said, lowering his voice, "Rowing is something special to me, Ma. Try to understand. It's a real he-man sport, and it takes guts and willpower. It sort of proves to a man what he's made of."

Jack paused again, trying to select the right words.

"In rowing," he continued, "you can let up, slacken off, fall back, at any time. The decision is entirely yours. No one forces you, the way a fist-fighter must defend himself, or a halfback must keep going with a football tucked under his arm, or a hockey player must dodge to keep the puck and shoot. It's your own decision. You have to beat and lash and hurt yourself with the sculls. The water rushes by, the slide hurts your backside, your hands burn from the oars, your back aches, exhaustion blinds you, your arms and legs are like heavy weights—but there's no encouraging voice beside you, no helping hand. You've got to rely on muscle and heart, on spirit and soul, on will and determination, such as no other sport demands."

Jack ran his fingers through his hair, and looked at his mother affectionately.

"I think you can see why I want to be champion," he said. "Rowing's the king of all iron-man sports."

Mother Kelly's apprehensions dissolved into a radiant smile. She did understand. She knew that her boy had to prove something to himself before he would be good for anything else.

"Off to bed with you," she said. "You have a race tomorrow."

Jack was a member of the Vesper Boat Club and was being sent to New York to row with a teammate in the doubles event on the Harlem River. Lying in bed, his mind wandered back a year or so before when he was just starting out and he belonged to the Chamounix Boat Club, one of the poorer clubs on the Schuylkill. Jack chuckled as he recalled his first trip in a four-oared gig. He and his mates, all green as the grass of Scotland, had sloshed down the river clumsily. There was an oar in the water constantly. They stopped rowing after a mile. Their bodies were as limp as old rags. Coincidentally,

George and Elizabeth Kelly had been out along the river enjoying a casual Sunday walk, and they saw the sloppy performance. They had no inkling that Jack was in the gig. They doubled up with laughter.

George, always the Shakespearian actor, struck a pose, and roared, "By my faith, sis, but that is a motley crew."

That had been Jack's humble beginning, but, as he was to discover on the Harlem River the following afternoon, it was only the start of his humbling as an oarsman.

Jack's doubles partner turned to him before stepping into their shell, and asked, "Nervous, Jack?"

"Naw," said Jack, shaking.

"I am," admitted his mate.

At the starting line, the referee raised his pistol to fire.

"On your marks," he commanded.

Before he could pull the trigger there was an awful commotion. Jack and his partner had become so excited they tipped over. The tide was swift, carrying them a quarter-mile downriver. The race officials had to send a rescue boat to fetch them out. The race went ahead without them. Jack returned to East Falls a wetter, but wiser, oarsman.

Jack was back again at the same old starting line six months later. This time he was entered in the junior single sculls of the Decoration Day Regatta.

Pushing off from the dock, Jack told himself, "My partner was at fault for upsetting us last year." He glided up to the starting line—and promptly upset! The referee boiled.

"Kid," he yelped, "haven't you ever rowed before?"

"Yes, sir," Jack said. "Don't you remember me? I upset here last year."

That was the end of Kelly's early-day mishaps.

Events took an upward swing for Jack months later when he won his first junior and intermediate single races. Ironically, Fred Sheppard, Jack's boyhood idol, by now a gray-haired man who sculled solely for the fun of it, was one of the contestants in another race two years later. Jack was hesitant about rowing against him.

"Sir," Jack told Sheppard in the boathouse before the start of the race, "I feel guilty about racing against you this afternoon. Why, in your prime I wouldn't belong on the same river with you. If I'm first and you're second coming down the stretch, I'm going to ease up and let you pass me."

The old champion put an arm around Jack's shoulder. His eyes twinkled.

"Son, I'm old and you're young," he said. "I can't keep up with you young fellows anymore. You go out there and win it—if you can."

He gave Jack a slap on the seat and left.

Jack, buoyed by his idol's sportsmanship, won in a breeze. And he kept right on winning after that, piling victory upon victory, winning every championship in sight. He was rapidly becoming the finest sculler in the nation, and he carried his honors proudly. His confidence skyrocketed with each victory. When newspapermen asked him to comment on his chances in an upcoming race, Jack's answer always was the same: "Oh, you want to know who's going to finish second. *I'm* going to be first, of course." That kind of self-assurance is the hallmark of all great champions. Jack got so plumb accurate with his prophecies that he practically put the 98% Wrong Club out of business.

Jack was far more than an individualist. He was a tremendous team man, too, an all-around competitor. Vesper Boat Club ruled the water from coast to coast in those days and Jack was now its leader and inspiration. No oarsman knew more about racing. He not only knew the times for his own men, he also knew the clockings for the other clubs as well.

One rival coach swore that Jack knew more about his opponents than they knew about themselves. Few matters slipped his attention.

It is a wonder Jack never killed himself from pure overwork. Beside single sculls, he was racing in the doubles, four-oared and eight-oared as well. He was all over the river. During his rowing career he won 125 races in open regattas. Stroking a four-oared shell one afternoon, Jack's side of the boat was stronger than its opposite side. He ordered the boat back to the boathouse. There he placed it on horses, dug up some tools, and bent the fin against the side. In this way he elminated the worry of the shell wandering drunkenly over the race course, despite the fact he knew he would have to work twice as hard himself to keep an even line.

It was the gray matter tucked under Jack's skull that made him a great competitor. He wasn't missing a trick. He was getting so good that he could quickly size up an opponent's strategy as the race progressed, rowing only as hard as he had to. Then suddenly he would pick up the beat and split the race wide open. He could be either patient or daring as he waited for the right moment to strike in a burst of fury and crush his opponent's spirit. He conserved his energy in the singles, knowing he would have to row in the doubles, fours and eights. He let the other man set the pace.

"How fast exactly is Kelly?" Jake Muller, Jack's coach, was asked one afternoon.

Coach Muller shrugged.

"To tell you the truth, I don't know," he said frankly. "But it's a length and a half faster than anybody else."

Jack had come a long way since his first big race on the Harlem. He improved daily, not satisfied just to be the king of the Schuylkill. He wanted that national championship, and, yes, even the world's title possibly. He had trained his mind to work like chain lightning in the heat of competition, and his body to obey with equal swiftness.

Jack had come to know the starters pretty well by this time, and he could tell at a glance exactly when they were going to fire their pistols. One starter held his pistol in his right hand and clutched his coat with his left hand when he got set to fire. Jack never waited for the flash of the shot when this particular starter grabbed his coat. He knew what was coming and was always off just a shade ahead of the gun.

A new starter turned up at an eastern regatta one Saturday. He was Elliot Farley, a former Harvard rowing captain, and he told this story on himself years later at a banquet in Philadelphia. Farley warned Jack that he knew of his gun-beating tactics.

"And no funny stuff today, Kelly," he said.

"Yes, sir," said Jack, innocently.

There were four or five singles on the starting line. The former Cantab, with a severe eye on Mr. Kelly, lined them up and, at the proper moment, pulled the trigger. All burst off the mark—except Jack. He sat still in his shell. The others flashed up the river.

The starter peered down at Kelly sitting quietly in his shell, and snapped, "What's the matter?"

"Is it all right for me to go now, mister?" Jack asked.

Jack still beat the others by a couple of lengths.

As he grew older, Jack's attitude toward other sports began to change. He knew that to keep in condition during the off-season, he should keep active. So he played football and basketball and boxed. He was a whale of a football player, one of the finest halfbacks ever to come out of Philadelphia. He played with a semi-professional team in East Falls. Despite Jack's powerful body, his father considered football too dangerous and a waste of time for a growing boy. Jack tried to keep his grid activities a secret from his dad, but it was impossible. He frequently came home covered with blood.

It is fascinating, in a psychiatric sense, that the greatest oarsman in U.S. history, if not the world, had to play football secretly to become such a well-rounded athlete. But how could John Henry Kelly know in those formative years that the boy he lectured because of his over-indulgence in sports would one day, because of sport, meet and chat with Kings and Presidents, travel the whole world, make a fortune, become an inspirational, international figure?

Jack's favorite hangout during the off-season was a ham and egg joint moored on one of East Falls' numerous bluffs. The boys called it the Gunboat. It was captained by a man named Ed Byrne. Jack enjoyed the atmosphere of the Gunboat because the conversation was liberally spiced with the patois of the sports mob. The customers were mostly athletes, and their intimacy with sports and its personalities provided a wealth of background material for animated bull sessions. The stories that bounced off the walls and deck had an abundance of what the sport literati in the back room call "the inside dope."

Pound for pound, and man for man, the Gunboat regulars could outfight a maddened bull moose, outrun a virtuous blonde, outjump a kangaroo, and outwit a con man. One of the star lodge brothers of this exclusive fraternity was Paddy Neilan, a fiery little Irishman who was recognized as the gay lothario of the Falls. He was a garrulous young man with a highly persuasive way of talking. It took more than a side show pitchman to talk down Paddy. When he held the floor, even Hercules could not pry it loose. Nobody matched his volume, stamina and gestures on even terms.

Paddy was a debonair chap. His flamboyant raiment bedazzled many a feminine eye. Nothing along the strand ever out-Englished the English cut of Paddy's pristine splendor, topped by a pearl gray fedora. Paddy and his coterie generally could be seen standing in front of the Gunboat, on the corner of Ridge and Midvale, each night, doing a bit of optic nibbling as the sweet young marshmallow delights passed by on their way home.

Another colorful character headlining the Gunboat roster was Pat McCarthy. He was a blustering Babbitt, sort of the prototype of Ralph Cramden, the Jackie Gleason character. With the light of deviltry in his eye, McCarthy was always getting the Gunboaters stirred up into a frenzy, his Celtic tongue constantly coaxing them into some kind of argument. He and Jack Kelly fought many a gory battle. Jack was never one to run.

One evening after work Jack was sitting at the counter in the Gunboat drinking a quart of milk, when Pat McCarthy began picking on one of the smaller fellows. Jack put down his glass, walked over to Pat, and tapped him on the shoulder.

"You sure know how to pick your opponents, don't you, Pat?" Jack said.

McCarthy wheeled on Jack.

"Suppose I pick on you, Kelly!" he snapped.

"Fine," Jack said.

McCarthy was a professional fighter and had fought many times at local clubs. Ed Byrne, the Gunboat's proprietor, could smell a fight blowing up as a bird senses a storm, and he cried, "Fer the luva Mike! If you birds are gonna fight get outta here!"

"What about Dobson's lot up the street?" said Paddy Neilan.

Jack eyed Pat, and said, "What about it?"

McCarthy was a loud-mouth, but no coward.

"Sure," he agreed.

Jack and Pat walked out of the Gunboat, and started up the street, followed by a hundred Gunboaters, every last buck of them always with a hearty appetite for a good scrap. All the way up the street wagers were made back and forth. As if by a smoke signal, word was flashed throughout the Falls that Kelly and McCarthy were going to fight. The Gunboat could see this coming for a long time.

Arriving at Dobson's lot, Jack and Pat hurriedly stripped to the waist for action, their eyes not once leaving each other. Kelly was grim, McCarthy cocky. The crowd tightened its knot around the combatants, urging them to begin. Jack needed no urging. His fists closed into a handful of knuckles. He sailed into Pat with both prods. Pat met Jack with a giant swing on the nose. Blood flowed, but it didn't stop Jack's advance. He had a tremendous physical capacity for absorbing shocks. Pat needed no psychiatrist to tell him he had involved himself with a real gladiator.

For twenty minutes, without mercy on either side, the warriors cudgeled each other. At close quarters Jack brought his abnormal strength into play. His short, sharp jolts and hooks carried a rib-cracking impact, and were bruising and battering Pat's pink flesh something terrible. His eyes were growing glassy, his limbs leaden, and he was beginning to waver like a cork on a wind-tossed ocean.

Jack rushed in and drove his powerful right hand to McCarthy's heart, followed with a left to the stomach, and then a right to the head. Pat dropped, spread out on the ground as lifeless as death.

"You kilt him, Kelly!" somebody shouted, when Pat didn't move. A look of deep concern filtered over Jack's face. He kneeled down and felt Pat's pulse. It was faint. For an hour they worked over Pat. Finally his eyes fluttered, and he said feebly, "Y-y-ya' had enough, Kelly?"

Jack heaved a big sigh of relief, seeing that his victim was going to be all right.

"Yeah," he smiled, "let's call it a draw."

This story is told to illustrate that the Kelly boys were taught not to be defeated, an old Kelly custom that began way back in knickerbocker days. Mr. and Mrs. Kelly let their sons fight their battles with other boys. Some mothers thought that was wrong, but Mr. and Mrs. Kelly didn't. To their thinking, it was nature's way of giving their boys the courage and strength they were going to need later on in life.

When Jack came home after the fight with McCarthy, mother Kelly saw the blood smeared on his face and said, "Was he a bigger boy than you are, son?"

"It was Pat McCarthy."

Mrs. Kelly said no more. If it had turned out that Jack picked on a smaller opponent, she would have whacked him on the head with that heavy gold wedding ring. She let her boys settle most of their own differences among themselves, and in their own way—which often was not gentle.

Although never a mighty billow broke over her bow, nor nary a six-pounder showed above her sides, the embattled Gunboat was in many a storm. Name any sport in which skill and brawn are standard equipment, and there in the Gunboat could be found a fellow who could meet the requirements.

Some of the country's leading golfers were nourished in the Gunboat. In 1920, for example, twenty of the best professionals in the U.S. were from East Falls. That was the year Jackie Burke, Sr., a Gunboat alumnus and father of Jack Burke of the present golfing generation, finished only a stroke behind Champion Ted Ray in the National Open. So jubilant were Burke's shipmates back at the Gunboat that they called out a cordon of police, put together a brass band, yanked high-stepping Eddie Clarey, he of the stove-pipe lid, out of bed—and marched through the heart of the Falls in the pre-dawn hours, waking up all of their neighbors.

One of Jack Kelly's most passionate cheer leaders at this

stage of his athletic career was Twin Prendergast, a pint-sized, two-fisted li'l son o' a gun who boxed professionally by the name of Joe Byrne. He was afraid of nobody. His hero-worship for Kelly became almost psychopathic. Twin saw all of Jack's races, even riding the rails and freight cars to Minnesota when Jack rowed at Duluth.

No outward manifestation of Twin's affection for Kelly was better demonstrated than when Jack got involved in a vendetta during an out-of-town basketball game. Fists flew. Local zealots swarmed out of the bleachers, closing in on Jack. Jack braced himself for action, standing his ground impassively against the mounting odds. Suddenly a loud cry pierced the air. Jack knew that voice. There was only one like it in the world—Twin! Assuming a MacArthurlike pose, the little fellow issued a simple, forthright command.

"Back to back, Jack!" he shouted.

Perhaps it was the ferociousness of Twin that halted the mob. After taking a serious look at Twin, the crowd suddenly appeared visibly shaken, and turned away. They went back to their seats muttering to themselves.

The Gunboat regulars followed Jack's career religiously. When he rowed on the Schuylkill, they'd borrow a rowboat and paddle over to Peters Island, where the finish line was located. They filled the boat with food and beer and stayed all day. Jack had become the idol of the whole town, and it was always "our boy Kelly" against the rest of the field. They believed him to be almost superhuman, and wagered huge sums of money on him. Had Jack lost, the boys at the Gunboat would have gone bankrupt.

Another one of Jack's admirers was Toots Shor, who was born and raised in Philadelphia. Toots used to carry Jack's suitcase to basketball games. He tells of one night at Madonna Hall. The game broke up in a fight and the mob of Madonna rookies were waiting to beat up the visiting team for which Jack played center. Jack said, "Get behind me Toots, I'll account for a couple of them before they can get to you." Toots, only a kid then, was always a hero worshiper of Jack's after that night, as he never expected to get out of the place alive.

It was at this stage of Jack's development that tragedy abruptly struck the Kellys, just as abruptly as it is being told here. One afternoon, Jack walked into the house and said he was going ice skating. Gostine Lake was frozen over and he couldn't very well do any rowing. Grace, then about twenty, and a lovely young actress, was home and asked if she could go along.

"Sure," Jack told her.

Jack and Grace skated together for a couple of hours, having the time of their lives, and when it was time to leave Jack thought he would try out his speed for a few more turns around the pond. He told Grace to stay behind and take off her skates. But she was as full of spirit as her brother was, and, unknown to Jack, she tried to follow him. The over-exertion was too much. Grace had a fatal heart attack, and later died.

After the funeral, mother Kelly said:

"The sun will never shine quite the same for me again."

All's Fair In Love & War

Time passed for the Kellys. Jack gained in stature and ability. He seemed to be a boy who was content with the rigorous life he had molded for himself.

Until he was about twenty-three years old, Jack just didn't go much for girls, largely because he never had the time for them. Practically all of his attention was devoted to rowing and laboring as a bricklayer for his brother P.H.'s contracting firm. Little did he suspect that he was now on the brink of meeting the girl who was destined to give him the happiest and richest years of his life.

The year was 1914, and Jack had gone swimming at Turner's Pool in Philadelphia with some of his chums. He had been minding his own business, when he noticed a young girl standing over by the diving board. He guessed she was about fifteen or sixteen years old. She was very pretty in a fresh, round-faced sort of way, with lovely blond hair and sweet blue eyes.

Jack walked over and introduced himself.

"Hello," he said. "My name is Jack Kelly."

The girl looked up at him and smiled.

"Yes, I know," she said. "My name is Margaret Majer."

"Where do you live?" Jack asked.

"In the Strawberry Manson section," she replied.

"I live in the Falls, too," Jack said.

They chatted and gossiped for about an hour, comparing interests and talking about mutual friends. Jack liked Margaret immediately, and vice versa. She was a gay, lighthearted young woman with considerable impish humor and many boy friends. She said she planned to enroll at Temple University and study physical education when she graduated from high school.

Before they parted, Jack asked Margaret for a date the following Saturday night. She said she was busy.

"Sorry, Jack, but maybe another time. Ask me again," she added.

Jack felt a curious sinking in his heart. There were times in every young man's life when all males should be exterminated except one, Jack thought. Saturday nights were the only evenings he had free. When he wasn't rowing, he was at night school taking an engineering course. Consequently his social life was pretty skimpy.

Later, Margaret couldn't forget the big fellow with the handsome profile, charming smile, and the smitten eyes. Her girl friends were asking, "Gee, Margaret! What did you do to Jack Kelly? He never looks twice at a girl."

But Margaret didn't need her girl friends to tell her that Jack had been interested. What intrigued and then bothered her was that she was feeling a little strange herself.

In this manner began the love story of Jack Kelly and Margaret Majer, a courtship that eventually was to last nine years before finally getting to the altar.

Despite Jack's newly-acquired heart interest, the world around him was growing dark and curiously threatening. Britain was warning Bulgaria, saying that Germany sought to disrupt the Balkans and enslave the states that played her game. President Woodrow Wilson was snarling at the German submarine warfare, and Congress was being asked for $400,000,000 to begin national defense, and raise the Army to 120,000 men. America was headed for war, Jack could feel it in his bones.

Then, in 1917, it happened. All hell tore loose, and Jack and George Kelly, along with thousands of other American boys, found themselves wrapped in soldier suits and kissing their folk goodby. Jack felt like all the rest. "Where do we go from here?" They had not been brought up on war.

Jack was twenty-five years old when the U.S. entered the shooting, and well on his way to becoming the national sculling champion. Brother George's theatrical career had advanced tremendously. Walter, too old for active Army service, was by now an international figure in show business. He pledged himself to entertaining our troops.

First, Jack tried to enlist in the Lafayette Escadrille, but lacked the necessary $1000 required to join. He only had a couple hundred dollars to his name. Besides, his family did not want him to join the French Army.

Next he tried to enlist in the American Air Force. That failed, too, because he couldn't pass the equilibrium test, which has since been abandoned. Finally he enlisted in what he thought was the U.S. Ambulance Corps, but quickly discovered he would be temporarily assigned to the University of Pennsylvania Base Hospital. Many ex-college football players from Penn and Lafayette were in the outfit.

The day that Jack and George left for war was one of the

gloomiest days in their mother's life, but also the proudest. She was a deep-rooted patriot. She loved her adopted country with an outspoken pride and devotion.

She told her sons, "This is God's country. It is the paradise of the working man. It's his duty to defend it."

Jack thinks back on his mother's teachings with immense pride. He had just about finished his packing to leave for camp when she entered his room. She spoke quietly, but her words carried impact.

"Son," she said, "I have read history books, and I know what soldiers do in time of war. Promise me you'll behave yourself."

"Ma," Jack said, reassuringly, "don't you worry. I think I would sooner die than have you lose faith in me."

"Well," she said, mollified, "if you don't come back and look me in the eye when this is all over, and say truthfully you are as good a man as when you left, I don't want to see you."

En route to Camp Merritt, New Jersey, Jack took a wad of bills out of his hip pocket. His life savings—$350. A soldier saw him counting his money and came over and sat down next to him.

"I'm from the Wildcat Division," the stranger said. "We're getting up a crap game. Want to join us?"

An hour later Jack's hard-earned savings had dissolved into small change. He'd had his first taste of Army life.

One of the fellows in Jack's outfit was Bert Bell, today the high Commissioner of the National Professional Football League. The pair hit it off warmly. The season before Bert joined the Army he quarterbacked the Penn football team. Jack admired his fighting spirit and leadership qualities. Like Jack, Bert had a weakness for shooting craps. Consequently, both of them were constantly broke. But their methods of recouping their losses were ingenious.

Shortly before shipping overseas from Camp Merritt, Jack

and Bert dropped in to watch a local wrestling program sponsored by the Y.M.C.A. In the heavyweight division a Man-Mountain of a bruiser threw his opponent easily. Afterward, the manager announced that the Y.M.C.A. would put up $50 to any guy who could stay five minutes with his champion, Cowboy Jones.

Bert and Jack rushed back to their barracks. There was a grappler in their company named Mike Dorias, fresh out of college and in superb condition. He had been a champion in school, and generally finished off his opponents in only a few minutes. He was just the man to lower the boom on the six-foot-four, 260-pound Cowboy Jones. But Jack's and Bert's problem—was Mike.

Mike was strictly an amateur. He disliked the professional tactics, though Bert explained that his amateur status was not in danger while in the Army. What's more, Mike was deeply religious, and wouldn't dream of wrestling for money. Jack and Bert decided not to tell Mike about the $50. In a way, it would be like a benefit—for a couple of poor but eager crapshooters.

Jack and Bert told Mike they didn't like Cowboy Jones, and as a favor to a couple of Army pals, would he climb in there and chop the giant down to pigmy-size? Well, since they put it that way, Mike agreed. The match was then set for the following night.

Mike sailed into the Cowboy like Injuns at Custer's last stand. A minute later it was all over. Jack and Bert, the winner's "managers," collected the $50 and were back in business once more. To this day, Mike Dorias doesn't know the great cause he had been fighting for.

A couple of days later, Jack and Bert boarded the Leviathan, largest troop ship afloat at the time, and headed for France. It wasn't exactly the Queen Mary service. There were 12,000 soldiers aboard. The aisles were only a foot wide and the bunks were like shelves, only eighteen inches apart. Portholes were kept shut as a precaution against anyone carelessly tossing stuff out and disclosing the ship's course. German submarines wanted desperately to sink the Leviathan.

With nothing to do but sleep en route, Jack was awakened one afternoon by Bert.

"Feel like fighting?" Bert said.

"Is there any money in it for the winner?" Jack asked.

"This is for the ship's championship," Bert explained.

"I'm no Mike Dorias," Jack said. "I'm getting only thirty bucks a month to wear this soldier suit, and I have no compunction about being paid for fighting. In short, Bert, I'm not interested in who's going to be champion of this floating zoo, unless the first prize is good old U.S. currency."

"As your new manager, I'll see that the winner gets paid," said Bert. "We split 50–50, agreed?"

"All right," Jack said, "but I've got to be there when the prize money is doled out to you, as you may be too near a crap game."

Bert convinced the ship's athletic director that a purse ought to be put up. There was a 190-pound Californian in the outfit with a good boxing background. Bert pointed out to the athletic director that the Californian and his man, Jack, would win their ways to the tournament finals. And without a cash prize, Bert stressed, his man would not fight at all.

Jack and the Californian moved through their preliminary matches like cyclones, just as Bert had expected. The Californian was big and strong, a stiff puncher, and he stepped into the ring against Jack with a string of impressive knockouts behind him. But with money on the line, nobody beat the opportunistic Kelly. Jack knocked him out in the second round.

Luckily one of the ship's officers, an ex-oarsman himself,

was sitting at ringside that night and recognized Jack. He invited Jack and Bert to share his living quarters for the remainder of the voyage.

Kelly's reputation as a fist-fighter spread like brush fire among the soldiers. In France, when he wasn't driving an ambulance, he kept in shape by boxing and roadwork, readying himself for the day when he would return to the States. He had only one idea in mind, to win the sculling championship of the world. Boxing was only a means of staying in condition, but Jack was proud of his string of victories nonetheless.

Stationed in Brest for a few days after landing, Jack, unnoticed, walked into his company latrine one morning and heard two soldiers from the Leviathan lamenting the fact that a "G.D. pill roller" had won the ship's boxing title. It was Army slang the boys had pinned on the Medical Corps. The medics resented it. Jack indignantly hit one of the soldiers a solid blow on the whiskers, then calmly turned to the other and said to tell his slumbering friend when he awoke that "Kelly is also the champion of this latrine!"

Ambulance corpsmen had to be rugged. It was no place for lightweights. Jack's unit assumed command of a small watering station, or hot springs, at Chateau Guian, a tiny village about seventy-five miles from the Front. The wounded were streaming in daily on trains and to find room the Americans took over what passed for hotels. Jack and his outfit worked around the clock, day after day. Trains were bringing in 600 ambulatory cases a day, largely mustard and chlorine gas victims. Jack was learning about life, and gaining a profound respect for people. He saw men and women rise to great heights, many times where it was least expected. Everybody, he told himself, has a certain amount of raw courage.

The Armistice was still two months away when Jack got a break. He was transferred to a spot near Tours to take charge of a forty-group ambulance outfit, which was to move up and back up a sector. Bert Bell stayed behind, so Jack was without a manager when he started boxing again. He sparred two rounds each with eight of his buddies every day. He'd be ready for any more money fights.

One night an officer walked into Jack's tent. He said he was the athletic director at Tours.

"Which one of you is Kelly?" he asked.

"I'm Jack Kelly," said Jack.

Utter disappointment showed on the man's face. "You're Kelly?" he said, as if it were a joke. "I was told I would find a big heavyweight. You must not weigh more than 170."

"I weigh 180," corrected Jack.

"Still too light," the man said. "The Frenchie we want licked weighs 225. He's tough, has knocked out his last four opponents. If I don't dig up a heavyweight soon those doughboys are going to run me out of the country."

"What do you pay fighters to box in your Red Cross smokers?" asked Jack.

"The equivalent of fifty dollars in francs to the winner, twenty-five to the loser," said the matchmaker.

"In that case, I'm your man," said Jack. "You won't find nine guys in all France who need fifty bucks more than we do."

The visitor shook his head sadly.

"Sorry, fella, but you're too light," he said, starting to leave. Jack, at his heels, pleaded for a crack at the Frenchman. The promoter stopped. "Tell you what," he said, "if I don't find a big lug soon I'll come back and lead you to the slaughter. It's your life."

The promoter returned the following afternoon.

"Well, I guess you're it," he told Jack. "I'm stuck. You will have to go in there against the Frenchman next Friday night. I hope your life insurance is paid up."

Jack called his entourage together for a council of war. Because they had all been transferred to Tours, no one had been paid for two months. They agreed to slice the purse nine ways, $10 going to Jack because he was doing the fighting, and $5 apiece to his eight sparring mates.

Jack climbed through the ropes unobtrusively. The stories he had heard about his opponent were no exaggerations. The awesome Frenchman reminded Jack of "Frankenstein." A beagle hound could have gotten lost in the hair on his chest.

The Frenchie's name was Pierre something or other. He must have had a hot date lined up after the fight because at the bell he rushed Jack as if he was anxious to get things over in a hurry. Jack backpedalled, sizing up the giant's style. Pierre filled the smoky air with gloves, but most of his wild shots missed the target. He was furious, and he was muttering to himself when he went back to his stool at the end of the first round. He had hinted before the match that he would make quick work of the American.

A buzz settled over the packed house. Jack had only jabbed and blocked, content to bide his time. He had his strategy all mapped out as the bell sent him into action for the second round. Jack danced around beautifully, making Pierre miss time and again. Then it happened. Jack drove a rib-cracking left stab into the Frenchman's midsection, followed by a jolt to the jaw. Pierre was plainly dazed. He brought one up from the floor, but Jack feinted out of range and fired a powerful right to the Frenchman's unprotected chin. The referee started the customary count . . . one . . . two . . . three . . . four . . . When the toll reached five the referee stopped and waved to the other corner to come and scrape up Pierre.

Jack spent more than a year in France. Army regulations forced him to keep good hours. He neither drank nor smoked, was unbeaten in ring competition. He went in a private, won a commission on the battlefield, and came out a lieutenant.

Shortly before the boys came marching home, mother Kelly wrote to Walter. She said she was worried about George.

"I haven't heard from him in weeks," she wrote. "He has been exceptionally good about keeping me posted, but lately there has been no word from him. He's the frail member of the family, and with winter approaching, I'm concerned. George is a cold soul, not strong enough for that life in the trenches. Of course, I don't worry about Jack being cold. I know if there is one blanket in France, he will have it."

Even in distress, Mary Kelly had a warm sense of humor.

Finally she wrote to Jack about his brother. The letter arrived the afternoon Jack was leaving for London to chauffeur a new X-Ray truck back to the front lines. She asked Jack to keep a sharp eye out for George.

Arriving at Winchester, England, Jack went directly to the motor pool to pick up his assigned vehicle. He was walking along the road on the edge of a company of soldiers when he heard someone call out his name.

"Jack! Hey, Jack—over here!"

Jack looked up. What kind of magic was this?

"G-g-eorge," he cried. "What are you doing here?"

"We're moving out of a Southampton rest camp for France," said George. "But why are you in England? The last I heard you were up at the Front."

"They sent me here to pick up one of those new X-Ray trucks," explained Jack. "But talk about miracles, meeting you this way. Ma just wrote asking me if I knew your whereabouts. It's as though her prayer has been answered. How are you, George?"

"Except for a cold, I'm holding up," replied George.

"Listen," Jack said, "as soon as you get to France try to get in touch with me. I'll try and have you transferred to my outfit."

After leaving George, Jack drove his truck down to South Hampton to catch a boat for France. An English stevedore, while hooking up the truck, didn't take time to put blocks of wood between the cables and the sides of the truck to keep from crushing the mud guards.

"Hey! Watch what you're doing," yelled Jack. "This is a new truck and I don't want it banged up."

The English stevedore resented Jack's interference, and snorted, "Where were you in 1914?"

"Reading about the Germans chasing the English all over Belgium," replied Jack.

The battle was on. It didn't last long, but the name Kelly wasn't very popular around the dock after that.

Jack and George met in France again just before the war's end. A soldier friend of Jack's mistook George for a sergeant when introductions were made.

"I'm no non-com," George said. "I am not even a private first-class." And then, with a hopeless shrug, he added, "In fact, if there's anything below private, I have an *exclusive* on it."

On the eve before sailing home, Jack and some of his confederates dined at a French restaurant. Among the gathering was a fellow Philadelphian named Charlie Smith who had enlisted with Jack. An omelet he ordered was slow arriving. While he nervously tapped his foot, Jack and the rest finished eating.

Jack looked at his watch. "If we don't want to miss curfew we'd better get back to the barracks," he said.

"But what about my omelet?" protested Charlie.

"Too late to wait any longer for it," said Jack.

Charlie fumed and made a break for the kitchen. "No wonder you frogs eat snails!" he cried, collaring the chef. "You're so slow, they're about the only things you can catch!"

Jack was down to his last franc when he got to Camp Dix,

New Jersey, to be mustered out of the Army. Now he knew how his Grandfather Costello felt when he came out of the Army after the Civil War. Grandfather Costello, while walking over the bridge from Baltimore to Carrolton, had put a hand in his pocket and found a penny. He looked at the penny, and then the river.

"Oh, the hell with it," he grunted, and chucked the coin into the water. "I'll travel without money."

Jack tossed his franc away.

The disbursing officer at Camp Dix issued Jack $60 and fare home. On the train, Jack met a soldier to whom he owed exactly $60—two sixes instead of a seven came up back at Brest just before their troop ship shoved off for home. Jack paid off the debt. Thus he returned to the Falls the same way he left Camp Merritt—flat broke.

Jack Kelly was a soldier of no fortune.

But look at all the fun he had.

Kelly For Brickwork

Now the nation was moving toward a period of sharp and radical change. Perhaps it was caused by an emotional hangover from the war, but with the transition would come a spiralling, dizzy, whirling planet of play, a flamboyant, chaotic universe of clashing temperaments and flashing clothes. The years ahead would see dynasties fall, nations collapse, politics change, dictators rumble, countries torn apart by revolution.

Yet despite all this, it was back to work for Jack Kelly. The young man still had a rowing date with destiny, remember? And there was also his business career to think about. While he had been overseas his brother Charlie had taken over his old job with P.H.'s company. Jack decided there was not room enough for both of them.

George, who had gone back to the theatre immediately following the war, stopped over at East Falls one night and had a man-to-man conference with his younger brother.

"You're not happy are you, Jack?" George asked, getting right to the point.

"No."

"You'd like to go in business on your own, wouldn't you?"

"Yes."

George's eyes brightened.

"I think every man should get the chance to do what he wants," he said. "If having your own construction business is what you want, I'd like to help you. I once had my chance."

His own chance. George knew the torment going through his brother. Before the war he worked at the iron works, but his heart was on the stage. His mother was constantly watching him. She could see he was unhappy. Finally, she asked him what he really wanted to do.

"Act and write," George said.

"Then go on, son," she urged. "On your way. Don't be eating your heart out in work you don't like, when there's something you're wanting with *all* your heart to do."

George had kept his job three months longer, while he took a night course in a school of dramatic art. Then he resigned and went to New York. Life for him, after that, was much brighter. He quickly adjusted to this new world, the world of grease paint and one-night stands. After tramping from one town to another in an obscure company, he finally hit Cleveland. Walter was also there, and they met for dinner.

"George," Walter said, "I play Dayton next at that new Keith House. I have never played there and you have. What kind of town is it?"

George screwed up his face in a pained expression.

"Missionary work, Walter, missionary work."

Next George began to write vaudeville sketches, in which he also acted. He followed these up with full-length plays, and his fame and fortune started to grow. So when he talked to Jack about going in business, he reached for his check book.

"How much money do you need to get started?" George asked.

"Not much."

"Would $2000 help?"

"It would help a lot."

"Then take this check, and if you find you need more let me know."

A week after the meeting with George, Jack spent another weekend at Walter's summer cottage. Word had reached Walter of Jack's plans to go out on his own, and after Jack gave him more of the details, Walter's hand went inside his coat and touched his wallet. The fingers came away warm and glowing—they were clutching a $5000 check.

"Maybe this will help."

It was a check from Victor Records for the Virginia Judge records. Jack was speechless, but his eyes sparkled with warmth. This, in addition to George's loan, brought his total to $7000. What's more, P.H. had offered to let him use some of his heavy tools. This really was a cushion against famine. Jack started to speak, but a wave of Walter's hand silenced him.

"Don't worry about paying me back," Walter said. "If you make money you owe me five grand. If the business flops, forget the loan. You have given me that much fun just watching you grow up to be a man."

Now it was Jack's turn. P.H. suggested he talk to Jess Otley, an energetic young man with a keen mind, about forming a partnership. Otley had been working with Jack for P.H. Jack went to Jess to discuss the matter.

"P.H. thinks we'd make a good partnership," Jack said. "What do you think, Jess? I've got the money now. Want to come in with me?"

A lump of muscle worked at the hinge of Otley's jaw.

"Listen," Jack admitted, "I know it isn't going to be easy at first, but I've already been promised some small jobs and we can use them for a start."

"I don't know, Jack," Otley said. "I know we'd get along well together during good times, but I don't know how we would do in bad times."

There was a pause.

"Tell you what, Jack. I think I had better stay on here with your brother right now, but if ever you need me, I will be ready to come and help you."

"Okay," Jack said. "You will be welcome if you change your mind."

They shook hands, and Jack went to work rounding up a crew. In those early days Jack was everywhere, out on the job supervising his construction gang, in other cities negotiating for new contracts, back in the office handling management matters. It was a struggle, of course, but Jack plugged along on what he called "Irish luck," picking up a contract here and another there and managing to chip out a living. He worked scrupulously, and meticulously. When he had a problem, he talked it over with his mother, who was uncommonly wise in the ways of business management. He respected her judgment. If he told her about a new contract he was planning to get, she didn't just say that's fine and wonderful, and that he was the grandest business man in the world.

"Sit down," she would say, pointing to the kitchen table, where they held their heart-to-heart conferences. "Now tell me more about this new contract you have your eye on. How are labor conditions? Is the job properly financed?"

Jack would nod.

"How is the building materials market?" she'd ask.

"I can get materials."

"It isn't that I know more than you, son, about your job. I don't know as much. But I'm not ignorant about it, either. If I don't do anything more but ask questions, that helps. Because when you tell me just how you stand, you tell *yourself*, too."

It was difficult for Jack to try to establish a business and train for the world's sculling championship, too. His zest for the title filled every one of the days following World War I, filling them with sweat and ambition and hope, in the prospect of brighter days ahead. His brother P.H., a sound business man, advised him to quit rowing and concentrate on the new company.

"Jack," P.H. said, "if you worked at your job as hard as you do at rowing, you'd be worth $100,000 today."

"That may be true," Jack said, "but if I win the world's championship you couldn't buy it for $100,000."

All the time Jack was adjusting himself to post-war life, George Kelly's fame as a playwright continued to grow. He was, and is, a bachelor, so his mother always kept a spare room ready for him at home. There he did some of his best writing. He was always calling to his mother to come and listen to what he was working on. He wanted to know what she thought of it. She told him the *truth*. She didn't praise what she didn't like. That would be no help to him. George knew that he was in her heart. What he wanted was her mind. She didn't tell him how to write a play, but she tried to tell him how his plays made her, just a plain sensible woman, feel.

If she couldn't help saying to herself, "No, that man wouldn't do that!" or, "No, a woman wouldn't say that!" she told George what she thought. Sometimes he followed her suggestions, sometimes he didn't. But whether she praised or criticized, George knew his mother had been honest.

When George got ready to try Broadway, Walter offered

to provide him some contacts. George wouldn't hear of it.

"Why not?" Walter asked.

"If I'm going to be successful I want it on merit, not pull," George said. "Thanks anyway, but I have to make the grade on my own."

It was an exciting event for the whole Kelly family the night "The Show Off," George's first major stage triumph, opened on Broadway. The germ of the idea for this production was born back at the Gunboat in East Falls. All the Kellys: Mother Kelly, Jack, Walter, Mary, Ann, and Elizabeth, and Jack's best girl, Margaret Majer, traveled to New York for the premiere. They rode the train from Philadelphia to Pennsylvania Station, then taxied over to the theatre. Mother Kelly beamed. As the taxi stopped in front of the theatre, Jack said to his mother, "Come across the street for a moment. I want you to see something."

Mary Kelly thought to herself, "Now what sort of foolishness is the boy up to?" Jack gently grabbed ahold of her elbow and escorted her to the other side of the street, opposite the theatre.

"What is it, boy?" his mother asked.

"Look, Ma," Jack said, pointing back to a huge, brightly-lighted sign board atop the theatre. Mother Kelly was silent, but her eyes spoke volumes as she studied the lighted words: "The Show Off, by George Kelly."

Jack nudged his mother affectionately, and chided, "Go ahead, Mary Kelly, hurt me, but you will be sorry when my name is in lights."

Tears welled up in the mother's eyes as a flood of memories rushed back into focus. It seemed like only yesterday she had reprimanded George for making too much noise play-acting in the house when she'd tried to talk, and he'd retorted, "Go ahead and hurt me, Mary Kelly, but you will be sorry when my name is in lights."

Mother Kelly rubbed her eyes, turned to Jack and said, "I'm ready to go in now."

"The Show Off" was an immediate smash hit. It received a dozen curtain calls opening night, and when the audience shouted for George to come out and take a bow, he refused. Backstage he explained, "The bows are for the performers. They're the ones who have earned 'em."

That was typical of George. He always has shied away from publicity and limelight.

"The Show Off"—in fact, all his plays—was drawn from real life. The characters in his works were everyday people the Kellys knew. His family recognized immediately who in the Falls he was characterizing when they saw his plays. Many of his best lines came from listening to his mother.

Mrs. Dixon, a local dowager in the Falls, was the central figure in his "The Torchbearers."

A neighborhood woman, who was a fanatic about her house, set the wheels to spinning in George's head and he wrote "Craig's Wife," a Pulitzer Prize winner. George has an amazing memory. As a young man, he studied people, observed their mannerisms, peculiarities, vernacular, et al. His microscopic eyes missed nothing. He could hear a conversation, come home and repeat everything that had been said, just the way it had been said. His niece Grace has inherited this faculty.

Though their personalities were different, George and Walter had one big thing in common:

They had only to look out and study real life to find their fortunes.

A Dark Day

Like everything else, sports were entering a decade of unprecedented prosperity after the war in Europe. Folks were to enjoy in the next ten years the wild hysteria engendered by Ruth, Dempsey, Tilden, Jones, Ederle, Sande, Grange, Weismuller, Helen Wills and countless others who could hit a ball better, swim faster and farther, ride a horse more expertly or wield their fists more devastatingly than the next.

It was just about this time in the story of the Kellys that Jack, his life seemingly on the brink of success, rich and full, began to prepare and condition himself for the 1920 edition of England's famed Diamond Sculls, the granddaddy of all sculling events. He swam, played football, basketball and boxed to keep his superb physique trim. At night he lay awake planning and plotting how he would win the Henley Regatta.

Jack was once again following his pre-war training schedule. Mornings he rose before dawn, worked all day, slipped into his sweat togs at night and rowed till after dark. As always, his mother kept his dinner warming for him and chatted with him while he ate.

One evening, sitting together in the kitchen, she said to him, "Son, thoughts are things, but they won't be things if you just think about them. You must work hard to make them come true."

"Ma, I'm not letting it go at just thinking," said Jack. "I made great sacrifices as a soldier to condition myself for Henley. I've studied every trick of timing. I have mapped out races against men I figure I will have to beat in England."

Mary Kelly looked searchingly at her son, his lips pressed tight, his eyes steady and determined. She waited a long moment, watching him as he ate, before she trusted herself to speak.

"But, son, don't you think you are over-training? Don't go stale," she cautioned.

"Those two years in the Army have put me in the best shape of my life," said Jack, flexing an arm muscle. "Billy Muldoon—you know him, Ma, he's the great athletic trainer —well, he says I am the best-trained athlete he has seen."

Mary Kelly couldn't help but admire her son's self-confidence.

"Why shouldn't I be champion?" he continued, matter-of-factly. "I can scull as well as anyone. I'm just as strong. I have made more sacrifices. I know it sounds arrogant, Ma, but I have built it up during these lonely hours on the river, stroking many miles in all kinds of weather, while my opponents sit around the house getting fat and dreaming up excuses why they shouldn't punish themselves."

All the while Jack trained, P.H. hinted that he ought to give up the Diamond Sculls notion and concentrate on his business. Whenever the question came up, Jack stood his ground. He wouldn't stop rowing.

"Ma always has said you are stubborn," sighed Pat. "It can be a curse. Stubbornness can blind a man to everything else, and only occasionally does it pay off."

Jack's jaw stiffened and his eyes grew serious.

"I don't think you really know how important winning the Diamond Sculls is to me," he said. "It's the greatest of all rowing events, and I simply must win. The war took two years out of my life, Pat. Time is flying. I won't get another chance like this. I know if I win the Diamond nothing will be too big an obstacle for me to hurdle later."

Pat reminded himself, "Boyhood ambitions can become a beacon." Looking at the set of Jack's jaw, he knew that his brother would be good for no one until he had freed himself, freed himself inside.

"You win, Jack," said Pat, with an expression of a defeated retriever. "Good luck."

Before the date of the Henley Regatta rolled around, Jack won the U.S. singles sculling championship again. Now he was twice national champion, and Russell Johnson, secretary of the American Rowing Association, told him to send his entry to the Henley Stewards.

"I have just come from England," said Johnson. "The Henley officials said that the war has changed some of their rules. They told me that your entry in the Diamond Sculls will be accepted."

Jack was so excited he marched right out and bought himself a new racing shell. He booked passage on the S.S. Philadelphia, carefully crated his shell, and went about cleaning up some last-minute business details before his ship departed.

A couple of mornings before he was supposed to leave, he bounced out of bed bright and early, ate his breakfast, kissed his mother on the cheek, and started for work. He was hardly out of the kitchen when he heard a rap at the front door. He reversed direction like a plucky engine and moved toward the other end of the house, for what reason he knew not.

"I will get it, Ma," shouted Jack.

Outside, on the porch, a Western Union messenger stood scratching his ear and studying the shell of his shoe.

"Cable for Jack Kelly," the messenger said, lifting his gaze as Jack opened the door.

"I'm Jack Kelly."

"Sign here."

For some inexplicable reason Jack always associated wires with trouble and heartache, and, closing the door behind him, he cast a frightened glance at the unopened cablegram in his hand. Staring at it, a grim shadow darkened his mood. He licked his lips.

"What is it, boy?" asked his mother, coming into the room.

"A cablegram—for me," said Jack absently.

"Well, aren't you going to open it?" she said. "Must be important."

Jack's heart jumped crazily as he tore open the envelope. Suddenly his body went numb. He slumped into a chair, as if in a trance, trying to marshal his thoughts.

"Boy, what's wrong?" his mother asked.

For a stunned moment, Jack didn't answer, then replied woefully, "The Henley stewards have rejected my entry in the Diamond Sculls. They're sending a letter to explain the reason why."

The blood rushed to Jack's face. He rumpled up the cablegram into a ball and let it drop onto the floor. He pressed the back of his hand quickly to his temple to restrain the impulse to tears. Agony filled his eyes, and he turned to his mother for comfort.

"I can't understand it, Ma," he said bitterly. "They told Russell Johnson I could compete. Why this cable then?"

Mrs. Kelly put her hand consolingly on Jack's shoulder, and said, "I know how much you have had your heart set on winning the Diamond Sculls, son. And I know how hard you have prayed for it night after night all these years. But it isn't going to do you any good to fret and stir and to ask the good God why he has said no. There is some reason, and perhaps some day you will find the answer—whatever is is best."

Jack knew his mother was right, but the streets of East Falls were like another country to him just the same that day in June of 1920. He felt like an alien, belonging to a faraway time, to the long, dreary mornings and nights and an inner voice that endlessly droned how important it was that he race at Henley, the dream of all scullers. His face was that of sadness, salty tears stung his eyes, and he felt he had let down the whole country. The air seemed stale and filled with an aura of human misery.

With the feeling of Poe's raven, Jack promised himself that there would come a day when he would wallow, humble, trample and laugh at the lofty Henley crowd. The memory of this rejection always would stick in his gullet, and he said to himself, "Granddad Costello, who really hated the English, was right after all."

Jack's disappointment quickly turned to bitterness toward the Empire, and he vowed to himself that some day he would have a son who would wear a replica of his Kelly-green racing cap across the finish line at Henley.

Jack quite possibly conducted the most intensive one-man feud against the British Empire that ever stormed across the pages of history. And when a Kelly feuds with the British Empire the result is a foregone conclusion.

Talking about his rejection to his mother later, Jack said, "Those birds at Henley never have written me that letter, Ma."

"What is their reason for not letting you compete then?" asked his mother.

"The old rule obviously hasn't changed," said Jack.

"What rule is that?" she asked.

"They won't let a man who has worked with his hands row against their *gentlemen,*" explained Jack.

"And why not?" snapped Mrs. Kelly indignantly.

"They claim that a fellow who works with his muscles has an unfair advantage over an aristocrat," said Jack.

Word, it later developed, had somehow gotten back to Merrie Old England that Jack Kelly was, among other things, laying brick. That was a bloomin' facer. In those days an artisan—a chap who actually toiled at a rough trade with his hands—might be a noble character and a dashed fine fellow in many ways, but he couldn't be an amateur for purposes of competition.

The days that followed moved along swiftly for Jack. Then one afternoon the load he had been carrying after his Henley rejection was lifted from his mind explosively by an item he read in the paper. He fairly sprinted home to tell his mother the news.

"Ma!" he shouted, waving the paper as he rushed into the house, "look here!"

"What is it, boy?" she asked.

"The United States is going to enter the rowing events in the Olympic Games," he said, pointing to a story on the sports page. "This is the first time our crews have ever entered."

"Now's your chance, son," she said.

Yes, here was Jack's opportunity to even that score with John Bull—a crack at the Diamond Sculls winner, as surely he would be England's representative in the 1920 Olympics at Antwerp, Belgium.

There were seventeen American scullers entered in the Olympic trials at Worcester, Massachusetts, but they didn't have a score to settle, and Kelly did. The winner would be the U.S. entry in the Olympics. Jack trained harder than ever to get ready for the trials. He worked out twice a day.

A week before going to Worcester, Jack raced Bob Dibble, the Canadian champion, in one of the most exciting sculling contests of all time. Their rivalry dated back to 1913, Dibble winning three out of the first four races.

This fifth meeting was at the People's Regatta in Philadelphia, July 4th. Hundreds of Canadians came down to the Schuylkill. All of their money was on Dibble. The shore was lined with 80,000 spectators.

Dibble, a regular block buster of a man, with wrestler's muscles and a boy's enthusiasm, stood six-three, weighed 195. Kelly stood six-foot-two, scaled 176 pounds. Dibble's coach was Nat Scholes, brother of Lou Scholes, the former Diamond Sculls champion, and he told Jack that the big Canadian was rowing better and faster than ever before.

Dibble got away to a fast start, holding a half-length advantage at the first quarter. Jack was sticking to his plan of rowing just off his opponent's stern. As they passed under the old trolley bridge which spanned the river, Dibble began to spurt, grunting between strokes: "Goodby, Kelly! See you later!" He shoved ahead about three lengths. Still Jack stuck to his pre-race strategy, without any bursts of speed in the middle. He'd save his bid for the last half-mile.

A half-mile from the finish line, the Canadian continued holding a two-length edge. The temperature was near 100, however, and Jack figured Dibble would soon begin to wilt. He raised his beat. He moved up. Now they were suddenly even, bow to bow, and stroke to stroke, with only a quarter-mile left. The crowd was going crazy. Both men were growing sick from exhaustion. Their faces were ashen color. They were stroking in cadence, virtually together, and pull as Jack did, he couldn't row any faster. The finish line was only 100 yards away. Jack released every ounce of strength he had left. But was it enough? He couldn't tell who was ahead as they flashed across the line. His head throbbed, his arms and legs ached, his tongue felt like leather. He couldn't see. He was at the exhaustion point.

Both Jack and Dibble rested silently on their oars for five minutes. Then the news was announced. Jack was the winner by a half-length.

It always had been Jack's and Dibble's custom to shake hands at the finish of a race, sort of a ritual. So they both started moving toward each other. Jack noticed that Dibble's face was greenish white. As the Canadian went to offer his hand, he collapsed and splashed overboard. Jack was in after him in a flash, but as he dove his shell's outrigger struck him in the belly, knocking what remaining breath he had out of him. Jack struggled to get his head above water. Reaching the surface, he saw Dibble's arm going down. Jack grabbed his wrist and pulled it over the deck of his shell, hanging on until the Park guards arrived to drag them both ashore. Jack recovered quickly, but Dibble was unconscious most of the afternoon.

Of such iron nerve and grit are oarsmen made.

Paul Gallico vividly remembers another instance when Kelly demonstrated plenty of courage, though courage of another nature. It happened years ago, back about the era of the Dibble incident, and the eminent writer says he will never forget it.

"For the glimpse I had of Jack Kelly that day afforded me a demonstration of the most marvelous example of self-control that I have ever witnessed in my entire days," testified Mr. Gallico.

"We were all oarsmen then. Jack Kelly was a champion, the best single sculler in the world. He was also as handsome and beautifully built a man as I have ever seen. I was a member of the Union Boat Club eight, which that year was the Columbia varsity crew intact. In those days we used to train from the Union Boat Club in the Harlem River and, when the school season was over, we rowed for Union in the Decoration Day Regatta on the Schuylkill River in Philadelphia.

"Kelly was there, too, wearing a green cap and preparing to sweep the river in the single-scull event. I remember how I admired him. He looked like a champion, walked like a champion, talked like a champion and later on behaved like one.

"There is a small wooded island in the Schuylkill, not far from the start of the race, with a landing dock for shells, and on regatta day all of the crews foregathered there with their slender, polished craft to await their call to the starting line in the long program of events.

"We rowed thither, picked the big shell out of the water, tossed it, carried it up the path and rested it on horses until the time should come when we would want it.

"The island thus was full of shells—eights, fours, pair oars, singles and doubles—all bottoms up. Kelly's was there too, and Kelly, in Kelly-green rowing trunks and cap.

"Kelly's shell rested not on high wooden horses, but on a couple of two-by-fours, and thus was low on the ground. I can still see the rich golden-brown of the paper-thin wood, and Kelly polishing, polishing, polishing. For the higher the polish and the slicker the surface, the faster the craft slips through the water with less resistance from friction.

"Oh, it was a beautiful thing, that shell, as fine a piece of craftsmanship as one could see, sleek, gleaming, perfect in workmanship and balance. Also it was a part of Kelly, I would say, an extension of him when he sat in it.

"The island was likewise full of spectators lining the shores and watching from the slight elevation as the crews going by fought it out.

"Somebody called Kelly away from his shell for a moment. I can see it all happening again, just as it did in the long ago of my youth, and it turns me a little sick at the stomach now, even as it did then.

"A race came by the island, coxswains barking, oars chunking rhythmically in rowlocks. A young hoodlum, heedless and irresponsible, pelted roisteringly through the area of parked shells in a rush to see the boats go by and put his foot through the bottom of Kelly's shell.

"I remember the heart-rending crunch of the wood splintering as the shoe went through, and the vacuous grin on the face of the boy, a particularly unattractive specimen, pasty-faced, flabby, ugly.

"And then Kelly came back.

"I waited for the explosion that must come. I waited for the mighty Kelly to knock him bodily out of the shell, lifting him skyward with a single mighty punch, hitting him perhaps so hard and far that, rising into the ether and piercing the earth's atmosphere, this monster would become a hideous but permanent satellite circling the planet.

"But there was no sound and no move out of Kelly. He looked at the ruined shell, quietly and contemplatively and with even a bit of unbelieving curiosity. Then he gazed at the boy, up and down. Finally, without a word or gesture, he turned his back and quietly walked away.

"All right. So there was nothing he could do or say that would have helped the situation; the damage was done, his boat staved in beyond repair, the race and medal lost. But could you have exercised such intelligence and self-control under provocation? I know that I could not, though the memory of Kelly's feat and the lesson inherent in it has never been out of my mind since.

"Remember that day, Kelly? Brother, you were a man!"

A week after beating Dibble, it was simply a matter of routine as Jack breezed through the Olympic trials in the singles at Worcester. He also teamed with his cousin, Paul Costello, to qualify in the doubles. They crated their shells, got their passports and visas, and prepared to leave for Belgium with other U.S. Olympic hopefuls on an old transport named the "General Sherman."

A few nights before departure, Jack lay on his bed and thought of Margaret Majer. Their courtship was fast becoming a problem of grave concern to him. They had not been seeing a lot of each other since he got back from overseas, and he knew he wanted to marry her. But first there were some snags to smooth out. Such as, he hadn't yet fully established his new contracting business. His sisters, Grace and Elizabeth, had died just before he went away to war, his father had died while he was away and he didn't think his mother should be left alone. Then, of course, there was the Olympic Games—Jack simply had to win that Olympic medal before settling down to marriage!

Jack's rowing and business had taken most of his time and no girl is going to play second fiddle to business or rowing. The relationship was a bit strained.

He had hoped they could get together and discuss things sensibly before he left, but now he was caught in the whirl of the Olympics and the clock was ticking on.

Love matters would have to wait.

Jack's Prayers Answered

On to the Olympic Games at last. It was a slow journey to Antwerp, but the thirteen days it took to cross the Atlantic gave Jack and Paul Costello plenty of time to plan their strategy and keep in shape by working out on the ship's rowing machines.

Each night en route, Jack knelt beside his bunk and prayed, a silent ritual he has conducted morning and night all his life. He makes his prayers a talk with God. Jack thanks Him for all the blessings He has bestowed and for the good health he enjoys. Jack mentions his plans, and hopes that his wishes will be granted.

Now, as he knelt, Jack spoke to God of a plan, and he laid it on the line. He asked Him to arrange it so he'd meet Jack Beresford, the Diamond Sculls champion, in the Olympic finals. Jack stressed how important it was that the Englishman's name be drawn in the opposite bracket to Kelly's. This way—providing both went undefeated in the preliminary heats, of course—they would meet in the Olympic championship finals.

Jack didn't think this was asking too much of God, particularly in view of the fact he'd spent twelve years training for the Diamond Sculls and then been rejected because he was guilty of doing honest toil with his hands.

Now, looking back on that dreary morning when the cable arrived, Jack couldn't help but think: "Whatever is is best, as Ma said. Perhaps the Power that shapes our destiny was only writing the book, sort of putting me through the crucible of life to see if I am tempered to be a champion."

It may be that God was listening, or possibly He simply had gotten tired of hearing the same plea, night after night, but Kelly's prayers were pleasantly answered. The Englishman's name was drawn in the upper bracket, Jack's in the lower.

Suddenly the world no longer seemed a stubborn conspiracy against the American champion. Now it was going to be possible for him to race the Diamond Sculls champion. He would show that Henley crowd!

The night the news of the drawing was announced, Jack got down on his knees beside his bed and stared out the open window into which the stars were sparkling brightly. "Thank you, God," he said, "you won't hear another request from me. You've done your part. Now it is up to me."

Beresford swept through the preliminary heats easily, but Jack, through no fault of his own, almost missed the boat. He was rowing against a big Swede, named Jungloff, a strong lad, in the first heat and early in the race his shell snagged a thick vine that was stretching in his path, slowing him down. At the 500-meter mark, Jack trailed by two lengths. He had to perform the neat trick of chopping away at the vine and keeping up his stroke simultaneously. Jack barely won.

In the semi-finals, it was Kelly against Hadfield of New Zealand, whom many experts felt would win the world's championship. He was an odds-on favorite to beat Kelly. Jack rowed his usual race—a half length behind until the last 500 meters and then sprinted and won by his usual half length of open water. This was the first time that the British experts gave any consideration to Kelly, as Hadfield had won the Diamond Sculls in 1919 and the Allied Regatta in which he had defeated all the best professionals. Because it was a service regatta, amateurs and professional scullers were allowed to compete together.

Well, there it was: Kelly versus England in the finals. Jack couldn't sleep on the eve of the big day. He tossed and turned in his bed, seeing visions of himself breaking an oar, or upsetting. His cousin, Paul Costello, who roomed with him, was no Rock of Gibraltar, either. They were also scheduled to race in the finals in the doubles. The strain had been terrific. Jack rowed the single each day at three o'clock, paired with Paul an hour later in the double sculls. The papers were saying that the gruelling pace was telling on Jack, and Beresford was better rested for the big event. His times had been almost as fast as Jack's and he had competed in only one race a day.

Jack wasn't worried by all the gossip. He knew down deep that he hadn't completely extended himself in the preliminaries. He had rowed only fast enough to win, saving as much energy as possible for the doubles event an hour later.

Jack reminded himself as he jockeyed his shell into position at the starting line: "Kelly, this is the only one that counts. All of those other 125 races you have won mean nothing now."

Jack's Olympic coach, Muller, reached down, scooped up

a handful of water, and gave the American champion the traditional baptism.

Cousin Costello paced the dock nervously, obviously more anxious for Jack to win the singles than he was for both of them to capture the doubles title later in the afternoon.

Thousands of eyes peered excitedly at the contestants. Everyone was familiar with the story of how Jack had been brushed off by the Henley crowd. It seemed as if everybody was there. King Albert and the Royal Family sat in the Royal Box with Brand Whitlock, the U.S. Ambassador, and dignitaries from the other nations competing in the Olympics.

In the Olympics, they draw a string across the course, which, in this case, was quite narrow. Then they line up the bows of the boats in case one boat might be longer than another.

Jack sat quietly in his shell. No emotion played on his face, no whims of the moment. "This is it," he told himself, "the championship of the world." He said a little prayer.

A loud salute by the U.S. Navy crew—"Yeaaa, Kelly!"—straightened him up. Beresford glanced at Jack and nodded. Jack returned the nod, then turned his attention to the official starter. Unlike American starters, this one wasn't using a pistol. He gave the scullers the signal to go simply by saying, "Avez prêt" (Are you ready?), and dropping a flag as he said, "Partez!" (Go). Jack had studied him during the preliminary heats and noticed that he had a prominent Adam's apple. Jack also saw that it jiggled when he was about to blurt the key word. The Navy crew bet Jack that the Englishman would beat him off the line, but they had underestimated their man. When Jack saw the starter's Adam's apple move in anticipation of saying "Partez!" he dug in and was off like an explosion, leaving Beresford a few feet behind.

Jack didn't want the lead, and he permitted the Englishman to creep up with his body opposite Jack's bow. That's the way they rowed during the first 500 meters down the course. Beresford raised his beat slightly, prompting Jack to press harder and hold his same relative position. Coming up to the 1000-meters post, Beresford moved again. But Jack kept pace, even inching ahead a little now, testing his foe's stamina and attempting to squeeze his wind. Beresford was fading, Jack could tell. He was breathing hard. His strokes were growing choppier.

At the 1500-meters position, Jack heard the referee shout: "Beresford! Get out of Kelly's water!"

Jack glanced over his shoulder. Sure enough, Beresford was out of his lane. Pain and strain racked his body. It was plain to see he didn't know just whose water he was in. Jack told himself, "He's used up all of his steam. It's time to move."

Jack knew that if he touched Beresford's sculls, the Englishman would be disqualified. But he didn't want to win that way, so he pulled on his port scull and pulled around Beresford. Jack's eyes stung from sweat. All his bones and muscles began to hurt at once. "Don't worry, Kelly," he told himself, "the pace is hurting Beresford just as much. So here goes the works!"

Summoning every ounce of reserve he had left, Jack forged ahead. In ten strokes, he was amazed to see he had cleared Beresford and was pulling away. Was Beresford holding back, feigning grogginess, saving himself for one last sprint? Jack kept his eyes glued on the Englishman, at the same time bearing down. "Harder, Kelly, harder!" he told himself. The roar of the crowd of 50,000 was deafening. Beresford was white-faced. He had nothing left. Jack seemingly had found new strength, and was pouring it on—faster . . . faster . . . faster.

Jack shot across the finish line a couple of feet of open water in front. Seeing that flag drop was the greatest thrill of his life.

Waiting until the numbness left his arms and legs, Jack rested in his shell for five minutes, saying nothing, but thinking, as he looked down at his Olympic T-shirt and saw the American flag: "Here's Jack Kelly, a kid from East Falls, Pennsylvania, representing the United States in the Olympic Games, the greatest sports show on earth. Here's Jack Kelly, who used to be delighted if he could hold Fred Sheppard's sweater, now the champion of the world. I wonder what Ma is thinking about all this?"

Jack could picture her right now, rocking quietly in her favorite chair back at 3665 Midvale Avenue in the Falls, wondering how her son was doing. Leaving the house before each of his races, it had become sort of a ritual for her to walk up to him and put the Sign of the Cross on his back, and say, "God speed."

As Jack and Beresford sat in their shells in front of the Royal Box in which the King and Queen and their family sat, Jack turned to the Englishman and said, "Nice race."

Beresford nodded, and said, "Great race yourself. Well sculled."

Now the band was playing the Star Spangled Banner. The crowd rose, removed their hats, and the American flag was proudly hoisted on the center flag pole, the English flag on the second pole and the New Zealand flag on the third one. Traditionally the flags started up together. The third flag stopped first about five feet below the second. Then the flag of the winning country drew to the top of the center pole just as the national anthem finished. The emotion inside Jack was overwhelming. Tears juggled down his chest. He would never forget this moment.

Jack thought, "Sport is a great leveler!"

The doubles event was only an hour away and Jack returned to the locker room to rest. Lying down, he suddenly felt a sharp, inexplicable spasm in the pit of his stomach. Paul Costello saw him flinch, and cried, "What's wrong, Jack?"

"Nothing," Jack said, with masterly self-control. "Just a little sick in my stomach. I'll be all right in time for the doubles."

The race was only a half-hour away. There wasn't much time. Paul wasn't feeling too good himself. During the singles race, it seems, he got so excited that he followed behind Kelly and Beresford the entire distance, a mile and a quarter, by trotting along the road next to the river. He should have been resting, but he had wanted to see the race.

Kelly and Costello had never lost a doubles race, but they had drawn a couple of rugged customers this time. Both the French and Italian doubles were waiting for them at the starting line. The Italians were the European champions.

Paul, a mild, affable young man, turned to Jack and asked, "You sure you feel okay? It isn't too late to drop out. We got what we came over here for."

Jack looked at Paul with wide-eyed alarm.

"Don't talk crazy," he said. "This is the Olympic Games. Nobody quits here. I got my championship, and now we are going to get you a medal, too. Come on!"

"But do you feel well enough to row?" persisted Paul.

"I'm fine now," Jack assured him. "The pains are gone. Don't worry anymore. This one's in the bag."

What a doubles pair they made! Jack stood six-foot-two, weighed 176, while Paul was more compactly built, five-nine and 165. They were the exact opposites, in personality as well as rowing style. Jack was witty and sharp on the repartee, Paul was more serious and silent. They appeared incongruous in a shell together. Paul rowed with his arms, Jack with his hips and shoulders. There was no rhythm to their bobbing bodies, but their oars kept perfect cadence. They did everything together wrong—except row faster than their rivals.

Jack's and Paul's strategy was to let the French and Italian boats grab the lead at the start. They would permit the foreigners to jockey back and forth up front during the first 500 meters.

Following the plan, the Americans trailed by two lengths at the 500-meters mark. The French and Italian shells were stroking beautifully. Paul began to worry. Since he sat afore and Jack aft in the boat, he could tell by Kelly's back muscles that he, Jack, wasn't straining himself.

"Come on, Jack, pull!" cried Paul.

"Quarter mile horses," grunted Jack.

Silence.

"Don't you want the doubles championship?" said Paul.

"Patience is a virtue," replied Jack.

More silence.

Paul's face grew redder and redder. At the 1000-meters position, he moaned, "The championship, Jack. This is for the Olympic championship."

"All right, Mr. Costello," said Jack, "let's turn it on."

In less than twenty-five strokes the Americans were on top of both European boats and pulling ahead. Jack knew that the Frenchmen and Italians had tired themselves out early in the race and now had nothing left for the finish. Jack and Paul continued to increase their lead. Way out in front now, Jack turned to his cousin and said, "Now, Mr. Costello, there's your boat race. Win it. I want to bow to the King again as we go by."

Just then an airplane buzzed overhead. Jack said, "Wouldn't it be terrible if that plane dropped down here and knocked two champions out of the boat?"

"What do you mean *two* champions?" panted Costello. "There's only one champion—I haven't won mine yet. Come on, Jack, pull. We haven't won yet!"

Two Jacks and Grace. Sister Grace was always her brother's No. 1 rooter.

Kell and teammate, only teenagers, bend on oars to win senior lifeguard boat race at Ocean City, New Jersey.

Champions congratulated. The senior lifeguard event at Ocean City was Kell's first major victory. He was only fifteen.

An all-around athlete, Kell was a star football player at prep school.

Father, 55, and Kell, 17, dueled it out here. "I stole the start from him," Jack, Sr. confessed. "He couldn't catch me. I never raced him again. So you can almost say that I retired undefeated."

Throughout most of his brilliant sculling life, Kell has had only one adviser—his father, greatest American oarsman of 'em all!

Early in her brother's racing career, Grace was always at dockside to wish him luck before he pushed off.

Jean Sephariades, of France, was done in but victor over Kell in final of 1946 Diamond Sculls at Henley. Kell was taught always to remain upright at finish of a race.

Kell winning preliminary heat on way to 1947 Diamond Sculls championship. He loved winning races by big margin.

The big one. Kell sweeping the Thames, six lengths in front of Norway's Carl Fronsdal, to cop '47 Diamond Sculls.

After the race was over. All eyes at Henley were on the American champion after Kell's dramatic victory in 1947.

Kell was popular target of England's juvenile autograph set during his 1947 and 1949 successful appearance at Henley.

Hundreds jammed New York's dockside to greet Kell and Jack, Sr. upon triumphant return from England in 1947.

After twenty-seven years of waiting, the name John B. Kelly finally honored the famed Diamond Sculls. Grace, Jack, Sr., Lizanne and Margaret Kelly admire Kell's awards.

Mayor William O'Dwyer congratulates young champion on steps of New York's City Hall.

All Philadelphia turned out for colorful parade honoring hometown hero.

And there was a "Welcome Home" parade at East Falls, too.

To prove that his 1947 performance was no fluke, Kell returned to Henley in 1949 to capture Diamond Sculls again. Here he trounces Neumeir, of Holland, in preliminary heat.

Kell way in front of Trinsey in all-U.S.A. final to win Diamond Sculls in 1949.

All-America Boy. Kell's appearance in 1956 edition in Australia marked his third straight Olympic Games. He placed third.

The champion in his boat. Kell has twice won world's sculling title, the U. S. crown eight times.

Among his numerous titles, Kell also was Pennsylvania State apprentice bricklaying champion.

Kell and wife, Mary, congratulate Jack, Sr. after City of Philadelphia named its Olympic swimming pool after him.

Mr. and Mrs. All-America. They met at 1952 Olympic Games, were married in 1954, are parents of two daughters. Mary Freeman Kelly was National swimming champion.

Margaret Majer Kelly was magazine cover girl in 1919, later women's physical education instructor at University of Pennsylvania.

Mr. and Mrs. John B. Kelly were married in 1924 after nine-year courtship.

The Kellys always have advocated plenty of sun, fresh air and exercise as means of keeping young and fit.

And so it went, all the way down the river to the finish line. All told, Jack and Paul teamed up to win thirty-five straight races. They never were beaten, hardly were ever really pressed.

Afterward, the King sent his private car around for Jack and Paul with an invitation to join him at his club. As they entered, there was an aisle of young girls throwing flowers at them. Jack turned to Paul and whispered, "Boy, if the guys back in the Falls could only see us now."

"Yeah," said Paul, "they would be tippin' their hats to us."

Jack accepted a drink from the King, causing Paul's eyes to bug out. He had never seen Jack take a drink before. All during his career the boys back at the Falls had tried to get him to celebrate at the end of a victorious season and break training. "Not until I win the world's championship," he always told them. "Then I will have a drink with you."

After leaving the King, Jack agreed to have another drink with the Navy eight which had just beaten the English eight in the finals. And what a crew that was—V. V. Jacomini, bow; E. D. Graves, W. C. Jordan, E. P. Moore, A. R. Sanborn, D. J. Johnston, V. J. Gallagher, C. W. King, stroke; and S. R. Clark, coxswain. The one with the King had sent him spinning, but now he really was in high. He had often wondered how he would react to liquor, thinking about all the drunks who had pestered him. Some wept on his shoulder, some fell sound asleep, while others, remembering insults of other days, got nasty and wanted to fight. Jack got pleasantly happy, not really drunk, but full of alcoholic confidence and general love. He even thought the Kaiser was misunderstood.

Jack hated falling-down soaks, and he quit before he made a fool of himself. He remembered in time that he was still representing the U.S., and he didn't want to become involved in any international incidents.

Jack returned to his room at six o'clock in the morning, the latest he had ever stayed up except when he was on duty in the Army. "Country" Moore, No. 4 man in the victorious Navy crew, came back with Jack. He and his Navy mates also had been celebrating heavily. Country wouldn't go to sleep, and he kept Jack awake another couple of hours.

A Plebe, only starting out, it suddenly dawned on Moore what an important responsibility he had been carrying as a member of the varsity shell. He thought of all the terrible things that could have happened to him if he had caused the Navy crew to lose.

"Gee," he fretted, "it would have been awful if I had caught a crab, or busted an oar."

Jack tried to comfort him.

"But you won," he said. "Nothing bad happened. Now go to sleep."

"But supposin' . . . jes' supposin'," drawled the southerner. Moore had a vivid imagination and it seemed to override Jack's sympathy. Soon he had Jack, himself, imagining the horrible things that could have befallen him, too. They spent the rest of the night, wide awake, comforting each other.

Jack had lost Costello somewhere along the way that night. The Italian rowing delegation thought that Paul was Italian. For a rib, Jack told them that his cousin was. They took him off with them. Jack didn't see Paul for a whole day.

Following the Olympic events, all the athletes went to the Olympic Stadium, where the King and his family presented the winners with their trophies and medals. All of the nations paraded in their Olympic uniforms, each carrying their respective country's flag. The King presented the first prize, his eldest son the second place award, and his next son the third prize. The Queen graciously congratulated each athlete.

When the King gave Jack his medal, he said to his sons, "Regard this man well. I rowed, and I know how difficult it is for a man to win the Olympic singles, but to win both single and double in the same Olympics is a feat that may never happen again." Then turning to Jack, he said, "Mr. Kelly, I will send you a special trophy, worthy of these victories, later."

Six months later the trophy arrived at the Kelly home; the figure of an Olympic Athlete holding a laurel wreath, with "Congratulations from King Albert of Belgium."

Jack and Paul and the rest of the American Olympic team traveled to Liverpool to catch their boat, the Carmania, back to the States. Pat Ryan, the big hammer thrower, was among them. When the Carmania stopped briefly at Queenstown, Pat took command of all the Irish who came aboard. He insisted on bringing droves of them up to the first-class lounges, and couldn't understand why the deck stewards tried to stop him from bringing third-class passengers to first-class decks. Pat weighed 270 pounds. He won all arguments.

The Black and Tans were in Ireland at the time, and there was no love lost between the Irish and English passengers. Whenever the British delegation sang "God Save The King," Pat and his confederates sang out, "Wrap The Green Flag Around Me, Boys."

More than 100,000 Philadelphians turned out for Jack and Paul upon their triumphant return home. It was the greatest rowing celebration the city had seen since George Washington crossed the Delaware. People from all levels of public and private life attended the mammoth, dazzling parade, led by the Police Band. They were all there to see "Kell and Cos," everybody's heroes.

The homecoming for the most part was Kelly. Beside mother Kelly, Father David F. Kelly, Assistant Rector of St. Bridget's Church, and ex-Sergeant Bill Kelly, of Boston, who became a close friend of Jack's when Jack picked him up on a stretcher in France, were all in the greeting party that wound itself through the cheering downtown streets. Jack and his mother sat side by side, as Bill Kelly piloted the large touring car through the swaying crowds illuminated by fires of red and green glare.

The caravan ended up at Fairmount Inn for a banquet. It was packed with familiar faces. About the only one not there was Ann, Jack's oldest sister who had always taken care of him during his childhood. There was an envelope waiting on his plate when he got to his seat at the head of the table. Inside was a poem, written by Ann, who later said she didn't come to the banquet because she would cry from emotion—"and that would spoil everything." Jack smiled as he read the four verses:

"Little Brother, years have sped
Since first I combed your wooden head,
Washed your ears and cleaned your shoes
And doctored every scratch and bruise.

"For you I buttered loaves of bread
And dragged you, screaming, up to bed,
Brought many drinks, told stories too,
When I should have lammed you black and blue.

"You were your Mother's pride and joy,
I'll say you were a pretty boy,
With your snubby nose and your toes turned in
And the bark was always off your shin.

"With your fingers sore and your feet all wet,
I wonder why we called you 'Pet,'
But looking back across the years,
Filled with their sadness, joy and tears,
Now seeing you so strong and tall,
Well, really, it was worth it all."

Margaret Gets Her Man

There was a letter waiting for Jack when he finally got home from the wild, whooping homecoming celebration. It was from Margaret, the first he had heard from her since their misunderstanding.

She wrote: "Dear Jack—I was happy to see that your ambition to win the Olympic championship finally came true . . ." There was more, but it was all very formal and impersonal. She gave no hint of wanting to see him again.

Jack's mother had come home with him, and, familiar with the handwriting on the envelope, asked, "How's Margaret, son?"

"All right, I guess," said Jack, tossing the letter on the table. "She doesn't say much."

Mother Kelly, a very wise woman about matters of the

heart, said, "Can't you see that she is opening up the door to you again? Now you trot right over and see her."

Jack shook his head slowly.

"After our last battle, I don't think she would want to see me, Ma," said Jack.

"Pshaw!" snapped his mother. "She wants to see you again, or she wouldn't have written the letter."

"You're wrong, Ma," said Jack. "Margaret wrote to me only because she felt that it was the decent thing to do."

"And the decent thing for you to do is to dress up in your best suit and go over and see her," said Mrs. Kelly.

The City of Philadelphia planned to sponsor a formal banquet in honor of Jack's and Paul's Olympic victories. They would be expected to take dates as their special guests. This fanned the flame of an idea in Jack's mind.

"Do you suppose Margaret would like to go to the banquet with me, Ma?" he asked.

"Of course," replied his mother.

Jack brightened. His mother was wrong about few things. "Then I am going to ask her," he said.

Margaret said she would be only too delighted to go with him, and with her acceptance the path of romance was once more smoothed for them.

Jack's construction business was improving daily, but Margaret had just signed with the University of Pennsylvania as the first girl physical education instructor of coeds. This meant that both were very busy, for Jack was working night and day to make enough money so he could ask Margaret to marry him. Consequently, they didn't see as much of each other as Jack would have liked. In fact, Jack guessed he was maybe fifth on her list.

Jack proposed to Margaret one night in mid-1923, and she later admitted it was difficult to get the words out of him. He fumbled and garbled and went through all the sweet agonies of a man in love trying to declare himself. Margaret helped him. She said she was practically finishing his sentences for him. She also said that he probably got the quickest "yes" on record.

Margaret selected the following January 30th as the wedding day.

The whole Falls of Schuylkill turned out for the ceremony, but only a fraction could get into the church. Paul Costello was Jack's best man, and he took full advantage of the occasion to repay his nervous cousin for the needling he endured during the Olympic doubles race.

Jack and Paul arrived at the church early and slipped into a side entrance to avoid curious eyes. Paul expressed grave fears that Margaret wouldn't show up, and when it was time for the ceremony to start and she still hadn't arrived, Jack was convinced there was some basis for Paul's fears. Margaret was five minutes late to her own wedding!

While Jack fidgeted, waiting for his lady love to show, Paddy Neilan made him a last-minute offer. Paddy had no romantic preoccupation with the fixings and trappings and old-lavender aspects of matrimony, and walking up to Jack, he whispered: "I can still get you out of this thing if you want."

Jack looked interested. "How?" he asked.

"Easy," said Paddy, "I'll yell fire, and when that mob in there scatters, you scram."

Second "Honeymoon"

Now it was Mr. and Mrs. John B. Kelly. Following a honeymoon in Bermuda, where they stayed at the Princess Hotel, which may have had a prophetic influence, the happy couple, he thirty-four and she twenty-five, returned to the Falls and set up housekeeping in an apartment on the site of the old Gunboat.

The Gunboat had since surrendered to the march of progress, but Jack felt at home there. It gave him a cozy feeling to dream of all his boyhood pals who had trod the ground there. Still he yearned for his own home, too. He had his eye on a corner lot at Coulter and Henry Avenues, formerly an orchard. As a kid, he had climbed its trees for apples and pears.

Eventually Jack bought the property, despite the fact the owner knew of his sentiment and charged him twice as much as it was worth. Next Jack got ahold of Ed Hoffman, an old friend who was a great oarsman and a fine competitor. Ed designed houses. He was one of the best sports Jack ever knew. They raced against each other many times, and though Jack won, Ed always wrote him a congratulatory message after every match. Jack learned a lot from Ed about how much can be salvaged from defeat.

While Ed drew up plans for the house, Jack surprised his wife with the announcement that they were going on a second honeymoon. She thought he must be joking. This was August, 1924, seven months after the wedding. They had hardly settled down. Then Jack explained.

"I am going to row with Paul in the Olympics again," he said. "I didn't want to, honey, but they need me. Our Olympic Committee says it is America's only chance in the double sculls."

"But what about your business?" asked Margaret.

"Jess Otley can run things while I'm gone," said Jack. Jess had formed a partnership with Jack in 1922, with brother P.H.'s urging. "We will only be gone for a few weeks."

Jack and Paul breezed through the Olympic doubles, duplicating their victory of four years before. A strange experience engulfed Jack shortly before the Olympics got under way in Paris, however.

There had been no room for oarsmen in the regular Olympic Village, so the Philadelphians were moved across the street to an old cavalry barracks. They were given rooms overlooking the street. They were unpacking, when a factory whistle started to blow. Jack ran to the balcony outside his room. Across the street, hundreds of excited people stood watching a house burn. The first floor apparently was afire. Upstairs an old lady was hanging out the window, crying for help. Everybody seemed to be yelling instructions in French at once, but nobody budged. The old lady pleaded with them to come and get her.

Jack leaped over his railing, scrambled down the balcony, and dashed across the street. The gawkers warned him in their native tongue to stay away from the flaming building, but Jack's AEF French was pretty flimsy. He barged ahead, saw that the stairway was still safe on the first floor, and, taking two steps at a time, dashed up to the frightened old lady. The smoke was thick and smothering her. She fainted in Jack's arms. Jack carried her downstairs and out to the street to safety.

Jack later learned what had caused the fire. High tension electric wires had crossed with house wires. With more than 2000 volts ripping through the small wires, the insulation caught fire. The moaning whistle that Jack had heard had not been a factory whistle after all. It had been a transformer.

Fires had now begun in other houses on the one side of the street. Jack worked fast. He broke the wire extending from the central pole to the houses. Then he ran upstairs in the same house again, jerked a sheet off the bed, rolled it into a rope, and wrapped one end of it over the wire. With a big heave, he broke the wire. Jack couldn't understand why nobody was helping him, but later he was to understand.

Everything was becoming like a fantastic nightmare to Jack. But the most fantastic elements were still to come. Running back into the street, a girl rushed up to him, grabbed his hand, and dragged him after her. Jack heard the screams of women and he went along. He found two women crying hysterically and staring helplessly at a man lying motionless on the ground inside an iron fence circling their house. Jack started in, but was jerked back by the commanding voice of an American Army officer.

"Don't go in there!" shouted the Army officer. "The place is charged with enough electricity to kill a hundred men!"

Jack stopped apprehensively, frightened—but there was still a job to do. The house was on fire. The two women were screaming at him to save the unconscious man. Jack hurriedly appraised the situation. Luckily, the gate was open. He wouldn't have to touch it. Slowly, watching his movements, he edged his way through the gate and reached the victim, who was lying face down. Jack carefully turned him over—and his face went white with shock! Eight of the poor fellow's fingers had been severed and were laying on the ground. No doubt when his house caught fire he had had the same idea as Jack about breaking the wires. But without thinking, he had blindly grabbed them with his bare hands.

Jack felt sick, realizing what had happened. A cold sweat broke out on him, and he murmured to himself, "There may be someone around here more scared than I, but I doubt it. I don't think anybody in the whole world has been as scared, my knees are knocking together." He fought back the rising panic inside him, securing enough strength to carry the man out of the danger area. He was still alive, Jack could see him breathing.

Jack was stooping to lift the man up, when Bill Hapgood abruptly appeared, as if by magic. Bill was a member of the U.S. Olympic crew.

"Wait, Jack," he said, "let me help you."

"Bill!" cried Jack. "Boy, am I glad to see you. Come on, let's get this poor guy out of here."

Being extra cautious not to rub against the iron fence, they carried the victim out into the street. An ambulance rushed him off to the hospital.

By now the fire department was on the scene, people flooded the street, and Jack slumped to the curb, exhausted. He shook with fright, reviewing the terrible danger he had just been through. It all came back to him in a flush of horrible visions. Such as, when he yanked down the wire in the first house, he threw his leg over the iron rail of the balcony. Suppose it had been charged? He might have burned off a leg. Jack shut his eyes tight, trying to forget.

Jack sat on the curb for another hour, waiting for the scene to quiet down, then got up and walked slowly back to his quarters. Later he learned that the victim he tried to save had died on the way to the hospital.

There was serious talk of awarding Jack and Bill Hapgood the Legion of Valor, but the French government, for some reason, never got around to it.

The next September, 1925, Jack and Margaret moved into their new home, a handsome fifteen-room building of red brick, with flags flying. The flags were three-cornered and belonged to their first born, christened Margaret but called Peggy.

At the christening, grandmother Kelly told her daughter-in-law that she wished they had named the baby Grace, after Jack's late sister.

"It's an old Irish belief that if you name a baby after a talented relative, sometimes that talent rubs off on the namesake," explained the grandmother.

"Mother," promised Margaret, "if we ever have another daughter, we will name her Grace."

What a remarkable woman, grandmother Kelly. She celebrated her 74th—and last—birthday in 1926, but her eyes and mind remained as clear as mountain air right up to the end. She seemed to have the eyes of a young girl, wise and bright as Christmas candles, deep with knowledge of the years and warmly understanding. Her eyes seemed to know everything. She never got old. She just got wiser and more wonderful.

The end came suddenly. Mother Kelly never had been sick in bed a single day of her life—except when her children were born, of course—so when the news swept through the Falls that Mrs. Kelly was sick in bed, sinking fast, folks refused to believe it. But it was true. The years finally had caught up with her.

The end was near when Mary Kelly asked Jack to go and get Father Bonner, her favorite priest.

"He is God's good man, and I'd feel better if he was here,"

she said softly. Those of her children who could get to her bedside in time fought back tears, but, raising a finger weakly, Mary Kelly said, "Don't cry over me, do you hear? God made His plan perfect. Don't let anyone try to break it—or He will break them. I want you to go on being fine, honest citizens."

She let her eyes slip over her children, suddenly remembering another moment when they were all together, a happier moment three years before. Her sons and daughters, their husbands, their wives, and their children had held a reunion in her new home at East Falls, this very house. The home, the money to operate it, and an ample personal income were hers—given to her by her children. Back of those gifts there was a deep affection and an abiding gratitude. But that wasn't all. There was also an extraordinary reverence, a tremendous respect and love. Her five sons—P.H., Walter, Charles, George and Jack—were all men of achievement. In age, they ranged from the thirties to the fifties. Yet they were like small boys at a party when they surprised her with the new house. Only ones missing that day were her husband, daughters Grace and Elizabeth, and her first John, all of whom had passed on.

Jack reappeared with Father Bonner. As the priest held Mary Kelly's hand, he turned to Walter, standing at the far corner of the room, and asked, "Walter, don't you want to come over here and stand next to your mother?"

Hesitating before replying, Walter's gaze was caught and held by the familiar big gold wedding ring on his mother's left hand.

"No, Father," he said, rubbing his ear reflectively, "this is close enough. I'm too well acquainted with that left hand."

His mother smiled, then closed her eyes.

Mary Kelly had gone to join her husband and children in the other world.

The Political Years

On the morning of October 29, 1929, two weeks before Grace, the Kellys' third child, was born, America woke up complaining of a terrible hangover. The end of the Roaring Twenties had arrived. Panic was running wild on Wall Street. Within only a few hours more than sixteen million shares were traded and averages nosedived almost forty points.

In the weeks that followed, unemployment mounted. Apple vendors and breadlines appeared in every crag and corner in the country. But "Kelly For Brickwork," with an assist from that inexplicable element called Irish luck, carried on. Jack and Jess Otley seemed to be weathering the economic storm.

One day, Mike Doyle, one of Jack's bricklayers who had been laid off because of lack of work, came in to see him. He said, "You know I'm a good bricklayer and if you had enough work, you would give me a job. Well, I need the loan of a hundred dollars."

"Sure, Mike, you can have a hundred dollars," Jack said. Mike answered, "Well, it's a good thing you gave me that loan, or I might have held somebody up, or thrown a brick through a window."

After he left, Jack thought, "This is serious when a good American like Mike Doyle, with a big family, can't get enough to keep them—something is wrong with this picture. How many more Mike Doyles are there?"

It was at about this time that the Philadelphia political picture was becoming a national scandal. It was strictly a one-party city. The long reign of organized politics under the thumb of the Republicans had plunged the city into a hodgepodge of chicanery, graft, inefficiency and maladministration. This unpretty situation was costing the tax-payer a huge sum.

Thinking about it one night, a flame of anger rose up in Jack. He was convinced that Philadelphia was doomed to civic mediocrity unless somebody took a stand. Politics, one of the utterly fantastic shows Americans have built up, one that no other nation can understand, suddenly had a strong fascination for Jack. This was his opportunity to strip off the hide and probe into the mysteries of this shrewd game.

One morning a Congressman friend of Jack's dropped into the office and angrily told him how his Party was putting the squeeze on him.

"I've come up for re-election," he said, "but the Republican chief won't endorse me again."

"Why not run as an Independent in the primary?" suggested Jack.

"I can't buck the entire Republican machine," said the Congressman.

"The devil with them," scowled Jack.

"Well, I can't do it alone," his friend said.

"I will help you," offered Jack.

"In that case, I will run on the Independent ticket," the Congressman agreed.

"I will campaign for you," said Jack.

Some weeks later Jack got up and made a speech in East Falls at one of his friend's rallies. Apparently he was not supposed to do that. The following week the assessment on his house was raised $10,000.

"How do you like that?" protested Jack, talking about it to his Congressman friend. "I have just discovered that the Republican boss of my district is also the real estate assessor. I guess this is his way of disciplining me for getting out of line."

"What are you going to do?" asked the Congressman.

"I understand if I will go over to his house and apologize and promise not to make another speech for you, then everything will be squared and my assessment will be returned to the old figure again."

"Well?" said his friend.

"He can go jump!" snorted Jack.

Jack quickly showed that he had the nerve to sweat matters out. There's lots of people with education and ability around these days, but not many with the kind of courage Jack displayed in the early Thirties. He was aware of his reputation as a scrapper. It was one of his most valuable tools. Now he was putting it to work.

Margaret Kelly didn't want her husband to get involved in politics, but despite her feelings, she kept silent. The rest of the Kellys spoke up loudly, however, hating like sin to see Jack join the political scramble.

"It is useless to try and stop him after he has made up his mind on anything," pointed out his sister, Mary. "He's always going at a dead run. It's as if he stopped moving for five seconds the walls would come in and squeeze him to death. Ma said that from the time he was four he was always trying to kill himself."

Jack did some investigating and learned, among other things, that there were only 30,000 registered Democrats in Philadelphia, a city of more than two million citizens. The Republicans controlled everything. They were even paying the bills for the Democratic leader.

"This must stop," said Jack. He was quite positive about it. He has never thought in terms of party labels. He would just as soon battle a Democrat as a Republican if he thought for a moment that the Democrats were perpetuating themselves in office by the tactics the Republicans were employing against him.

One Philadelphia newspaper was shouting to the roof tops for a two-party system. Jack went to see the Democratic leader.

"Are you willing to break from the Republicans and help build a real Democratic Party here?" Jack asked.

The Democratic chief eyed Kelly coldly.

"Not a chance, Kelly," he said. The tone of his voice was poisonous. Jack sizzled.

"In that case," he warned, "I am going to try and take the Party away from you."

The Democratic leader appeared unmoved.

"Go ahead and try," he challenged. When two Irishmen disagree, something usually happens. In this case it happened fast. Quicker than you can spell K-E-L-L-Y, Jack was chairman of the Independent Democratic Party of Philadelphia. Now it was every man for himself.

George Eliot said that any coward can fight a battle when he's sure of winning, but give her the man who has the pluck to fight when he is certain of losing. Jack Kelly had plenty of pluck. He had been a registered Republican so long that the very thought of bolting to the other side excited him. He had heard the Democrats make so many speeches on a return to Jeffersonian principles, he was downright curious to try and find out just what Jeffersonian principles were. He didn't precisely know whether it was an oratorical topic, or an economic condition.

Another thing about the Philadelphia Democrats in those days, they were fighting among themselves so much that comedians were saying they were the only people on earth that would give a dinner and then couldn't decide who would be toastmaster until they all got to the dinner and fought over it. No job was too small for them to split over.

"No doubt," Jack told himself, "I've taken on a big job." One of his first moves was to try and get a lot of committeemen elected. They, in turn, then could elect enough ward leaders whose combined pressure would oust the old Democratic chief and put Kelly in. Jack's friends argued until they collapsed to dissuade him from carrying out his plan. They warned that his political opponents would smash his business, and him with it, if he continued to buck the Machine.

"Jack," they pleaded, "get out of politics before you get hurt. There's very little dignity, very little sportsmanship, or very little anything in politics."

By now Jack's wife wanted him to quit, too.

"A family needs a father around it," she told him. "Jack, it isn't right for me to have to raise the children alone."

"You're right, of course, honey," Jack said, "but I feel it is my duty to go ahead with this campaign."

Margaret Kelly said nothing and walked away. The scene was repeated night after night. Always it turned out the same: Jack wouldn't quit until he had cleaned up Philadelphia's political mess.

As a competitor in anything, Kelly's philosophy always has been essentially simple: "Let's go, and see who quits first."

Philadelphians had all but forgotten even how to spell

Democrats when Kelly initiated his platform. Jack had a pioneering job on his hands. He discovered that the patient had been sick with an acute case of appendicitis. Folks had a dim recollection that the D-E-M-O-C-R-A-T-S were a kind of semi-heathen tribe, a nomad race. They could live on practically nothing because they had never had much.

Kelly breathed new life into the dormant patient. The boys in the Democratic clinic decided that the Party hadn't had appendicitis after all. It was really only a stubborn case of cramp colic. A strong, healthy guy like Jack could shake it off.

Voters didn't know how to react to Kelly at first. He was refreshing and different. He was plain-spoken, and didn't mess with long adjectives and nouns like his opponents. He got to the point with facts, instead of the customary rhetoric and theories that gave listeners cabbage ears. Jack was not one to go around scenting up folks to win a vote. He shunned the whitewash, prettied-up tactics employed by his opponents. In fact, he lost the support of the toupee vote because of this get-to-the-point manner. During a campaign speech, he sought for a metaphor to get across the idea that one of his opponents had made an awkward *faux pas* to deceive the public.

In a fit of anger, Jack shouted, "He reminds me very much of a man who wears a toupee. The only one he is fooling is himself."

Touche!

Kelly suddenly found new allies in those Republicans who were also dissatisfied with the way their Party was being run by the men at the top. It was decided to make up a coalition ticket of two Democrats and two Republicans. The move paid off. The Independent Democratic Party won an election. This only four months after Kelly entered politics! They put in office the City Treasurer, the Comptroller, the Coroner, and the Register of Wills. They also elected a couple of Judges and Magistrates, plus enough Committeemen so that Kelly could replace the old Democratic leader.

And there was Jack Kelly—a political boss! By self-admission, there wasn't a political boss in the whole United States who knew *less* about the job than John Brendan Kelly.

But what Jack Kelly lacked in background he more than made up with enthusiasm. He was a hard-fisted leader, a strict realist, and a stern debunker of phony piety. He cleaned house.

Jack found himself being hailed as a sort of Galahad—the pure knight in a land of political dragons. The Democrats were banking on him to become a Moses and lead them out of the wilderness. Such talk, Jack knew, would put him on the spot. Sure enough, he became a high-priority target. Even certain national Republican elements, which never before had deigned to take him seriously, began paying special attention to Honest Jack.

The early Thirties were important years for the Democrats. They had a lot of catching up to do. The National Party leaders were telling Mr. and Mrs. America what they would do if they got the farmer's ballot. The Republicans had a bigger job. They had to promise what they would do—and also explain why they hadn't already done it.

The depression was at its height when Jim Farley named Kelly Federal patronage dispenser of Philadelphia. Immediately everybody wanted Jack to get him a job.

"When 1934, a gubernatorial year, rolled around, I started planning a campaign," Jack said. "I knew our organization of workers was weak. I didn't know whom to trust at first, so I got sixteen young, smart and energetic fellows together and organized 'Kelly's Flying Squadron.' Each man was assigned a number of wards to cover. They were to keep me posted on what was happening. The ward leaders, many of them holdovers from the old guard, didn't like my Flying Squadron because it kept them on their toes. Changes had to be made, but the organization began to show signs of coming alive. The Republicans were becoming increasingly aware that in our new lease on life they faced a formidable opponent. They were certain of it when, in 1934, we elected George Earle the governor of Pennsylvania—the first Democrat to win the job in fifty years!" Of course, the Democrats didn't win Philadelphia—but the Republicans did not get their usual landslide, which helped to elect the governor.

The Democrats had to run somebody for mayor of Philadelphia in 1935 and it had to be either a very brave or a very reckless gent. There hadn't been a Democratic mayor of Philadelphia in fifty-four years. Kelly, of course, was picked as the brave gent. In his campaign, he came out boldly for a general housecleaning of City Hall so that Philadelphia would no longer be corrupt.

Kelly pulled out all of the stops in his campaign. He never ducked around corners or hid behind the barn to cover up anything he said or did. He stood right out in the open and said, "This is the way I am, like it or lump it. I won't promise anything I don't think I can deliver."

In the fire and brimstone of the 1935 race, Jack took it as well as dished it out. A local columnist, supporting the Republican candidate, piled on the heckleberry. He kept calling Kelly, who has always been an impeccably groomed man, "The handsome Adonis of East Falls." After weeks of this, Jack wrote the columnist a letter with all the outraged dignity of a cat caught in a bathtub.

"I may be the Adonis of East Falls," he wrote, "but every time I think of the way you look it reminds me of an unmade bed."

Kelly's political experiences taught him much. They taught him, for example, that there's nothing as stubborn as a Party newspaper—Republican or Democratic. Voters are first to forget campaign speeches and Party manners; newspapers are the last. Kelly soon discovered his opponents digging through old newspapers and confronting him with statements he had made in past campaigns. Admittedly, some of it sounded like the old mandamus potatoes, but that was politics. Conditions and events change fast. What's good for the people today is ridiculous tomorrow. Consequently, Kelly's opponents tried all sorts of character assassination on him, but none of it worked. Some of the big wigs of the Republican Party hired a detective agency and paid them $25,000 to get something on Kelly. He was costing them too much money to win an election. They used dictaphones and tapped telephones, but were never able to get anything on him.

In the final days of the 1935 race, the campaign manager for Kelly's opponent went all the way and called Jack "an unmitigated liar." A reporter rushed over to Kelly's office to get his response. "What have you got to say about it?" queried the reporter.

"I don't believe he said it," Kelly said coolly. "In the first place, he can't pronounce or spell *unmitigated.*"

Kelly hit the Republicans over the head with everything but an oar, but when they counted up the votes his opponent, S. Davis Wilson, was the people's choice. The old, established Republican machine had been too much to buck. The incredible thing, however, was the fact that Jack polled more than 330,000 votes. He lost only by 40,000! This in the city where Democratic was a naughty word. The previous Democratic candidate got a total of a mere 31,000 votes.

It was indeed a moral victory for Kelly.

"We should have had Kelly row instead of run for it," one Democrat said. "He'd have won by nine dozen miles."

Kelly took his defeat as you knew he would—graciously. Thoroughbreds don't alibi. The following day the Philadelphia Evening Ledger, a Republican newspaper that had op-posed Kelly, devoted its editorial page to the loser instead of the winner:

"John B. Kelly persuades us to be a Democrat—his kind. For champion sportsmanship we commend to losers of all time Mr. Kelly's statement after Tuesday's election. The shining part of it is that he meant it.

" 'The Kellys,' he said, 'can take it.' And the rest was no stiff-lipped effort to put on a good front in the face of defeat. It was in keeping with his assurance that his philosophy of life is, 'Whatever is, is best.' With that he went on with a bit of verse that would be any real sportsman's creed:

Well, you are beaten to earth,
What about that?
Get up with a smiling face.
It's nothing against you to fall down flat,
But to lie there—that's disgrace.
The harder you're thrown, the higher you bounce,
Be proud of your blackened eye.
It's not the fact that you're licked that counts,
But, how did you fight and why.

"Well," continued the Evening Ledger editorial, "those are good words, but another man's. Yet the rest he added were his and also good:

" 'I do hope I am giving you the impression that I am a good loser as that is what I am trying to convey. I needn't tell you I am disappointed, as I would like to have had a chance to show you what I could do. But you, the people, have willed otherwise. I accept that with the knowledge that every disappointment I have had in my life has been only the stepping stone to greater triumph.'

"Whatever John B. Kelly may do after this, he'll never register a finer triumph than that."

Starting in 1939, tremendous pressure began to gather to make Jack run for Senator in 1940, on the same ticket with Roosevelt. When Walter Kelly heard about it, he took Jack to one side and told him to get out of politics once and for all.

"It's an ugly game, Jack," said Walter. "If you don't heed my advice, I'll take you for a ride, before the politicians do."

The next time Jack saw Walter, the beloved "Virginia Judge" was flat on his back in bed, dying. The end came suddenly, without any notice. This was in 1939. Walter, then 64, just took sick one day and dropped into a coma. Regaining consciousness, Walter, who had spent the last couple of years performing in movies, doing some plays, and taking life easy with cronies from the sports world, refused to be moved until brother Jack had been informed.

Jack got on a plane and flew to the Coast immediately. When Walter saw him coming, he said, "Jack, take me back to the Falls. I want to see the old gang again."

Knowing that his brother was dying, Jack put him on a plane and flew him back home. Two days later, life's gentle evening closed in on Walter, calm, serene and unafraid, but before he shut his eyes he turned to Jack and said:

"Life has been kind to me, but, Jack, there are certain things about living too long. I've been to the top. It is all downhill from now on. Remember, I have bowed to laughing millions, had my share of grief and glories, and when I bend the knee to whatever gods there be, I hope they are fond of stories."

Walter Kelly was a trouper all the way.

Whether or not it was Walter's influence, Jack, despite the fact that 187 of the 206 delegates were pledged for him for Senator at the state meeting a few months later, quit the political ring. His enthusiasm was gone. He trained Jim Clark to take over his post, then resigned. Democrats tried to make him change his mind, but he wouldn't.

Looking back on those last eight years, Jack admitted to his wife: "They were the eight hardest years of my life. They took more of a toll out of me than any of the others. I'm happy it is over, but I have succeeded in building up a two-party system in this town—it was needed badly and from now on we will get better government."

There was genuine sincerity in his face when he said it. You knew he meant it.

Chip Off The Old Brick

A new generation of Kellys started to come alive in the mid-Thirties. There was Peggy, the oldest, then Jack, Jr., Grace, and finally baby Lizanne.

When Jack, Jr. was born, in 1927, he was formally christened John B. Kelly, but his father, a proud man, would not permit the youth to be called "Junior." He said that his only son must be an individual—with a nickname of his own. Subsequently the boy always has been known as "Kell" by members of the family and intimate friends.

So as "Kell," the hero of one of America's most dramatic sport legends began to take shape.

One night, when Kell was four, his family was entertaining dinner guests. One of the lady guests asked him what he wanted to be when he grew up. Kell spoke loud and clear.

"When I get big," he sung out, sticking his little chest out like a toy soldier, "I'm gonna be an oarsman and a bricklayer —like my dad."

The other guests chuckled in mild amusement at Kell's outburst of pride. But he meant what he said. It was the honest truth, and the words tasted fresh to his tongue.

"That's my boy," beamed Jack, Sr., by now a millionaire. "I had to work for a living. So will Kell."

As the years ticked on, Kell's boyhood ambition became less and less a standard joke to friends. He was, they soon realized, serious about filling his father's seven league boots. He was becoming a veritable chip off the old brick.

Jack, Sr., had vowed in 1920 that he would show the punting crowd of Harrow, Eton, Cambridge, et al, that it was no dishonor to work with his hands, that a man can rise to business and social prominence in the greatest of nations. He had also resolved, God willing, that the name John B. Kelly would some day honor the Diamond Sculls.

Jack never asked much of his son—all he asked was that he grow up into a husky young man and put the name of John B. Kelly on England's Diamond Sculls, emblematic of the world's championship. Kell began rowing when he was seven! How well he remembers that first day, a day which was to eventually shape his whole life.

His father had come home from the office early and said, "Kell, how'd you like to take a spin with me in a boat this afternoon?" Kell looked at his dad, and his dad looked back. There was an odd light in Jack Kelly's eyes. Kell had ridden in a gig with his father before, but somehow he could sense that this was going to be a new adventure.

Mrs. Kelly, who had overheard the question, walked into the room and said, "Wait, Jack, there's no great rush about starting Kell on the oars. He's not old enough yet."

Jack sighed.

"Dearie, it's only going to be a test workout," he said. "I just want to let him get a feel of the thing. How about it, son?"

"Sure, dad."

They drove out to the Schuylkill River, changed into rowing trunks, and then walked down to the river's edge, where a two-seated shell was waiting for them. Jack turned to Kell.

"Son," he instructed, "do just what I do. We'll go slow for now, but when I bend you bend. Bend from the hips. Never overreach—like this—and avoid going back too far at the end of the stroke. Try to catch the water with your oars slightly inclined—like this—and pull the stroke through from beginning to end, bringing the blades cleanly out of the water at right angles and with a snap—like this. Don't hang when the stroke is finished, but let the hands drop and shoot the arms forward fast. Now do you think you can remember all that?"

Kell nodded. "I will try," he said.

"Come on, then."

It was awkward for Kell at first, but he had heard his dad discuss rowing so much around the dinner table at home that he quickly caught on. His father studied him like a hawk.

"Stroke . . . stroke . . . stroke," he chanted. "Keep your oars as close to the water as possible on the recovery without splashing . . . pull, pull, pull . . . don't drop your shoulders and kink your back . . . stop pulling up to meet the handles of your oars . . . stroke, stroke, stroke . . . keep your oar in the water as long as possible . . ."

After fifteen minutes, Jack said, "That's enough for today. You did all right, son. Good work."

They changed back into their street clothes and drove home. Margaret Kelly was at the door to meet them.

"Well, how did it go?" she asked. "Do you still want to be an oarsman, Kell—like your father?"

"It was fun, Mom," said Kell.

Jack smiled proudly. "Margaret," he said, "I think we have bred ourselves another champion. He's a natural if I ever saw one."

"Well, he should be," Margaret Kelly said. "Look who his coach is."

They both laughed.

After that, Jack and Kell became familiar sights on the Schuylkill, creating mingled feelings of compassion and respect. Folks passing by, thoroughly acquainted with the legend of how Jack Kelly had been brushed off by the English, would watch Kell tug laboriously on the blades and say, "Wonderful boy. Just like his dad. After all these years, wouldn't it be great if he could go over there to England and win the Diamond Sculls for his dad. That would be some sort of poetic justice."

Jack brought Kell along carefully and properly. When the lad started, he didn't have a new shell. He began learning with a second-hand midget rowboat, about eight feet long, and Jack would take him down to Ocean City and let him paddle around in that. As he progressed, he earned better equipment. Jack wanted Kell to know what these advances meant and to appreciate them. Kell never complained. His father would watch him and say to himself, "There's great stuff in the boy." Kell was getting the same hard tutoring that experience had given his father.

Besides teaching Kell the tricks of rowing, Jack also preached to him the laws of the sea.

"Son," Jack said one day, "you must always respect the ocean. Be cautious out there. It is more powerful than you."

Kell said nothing. He was only about eight years old at the time, and he really didn't quite understand what his father meant.

"Come on," Jack said, "let's go fishing."

They were spending the summer at Ocean City, and Jack

and young Kell piled into a rowboat and started out for deeper waters. They had been fishing for about an hour when suddenly, from off in the distance, Jack spotted what looked like a human body, floating in the water. The paper had mentioned something a couple of nights before about two small brothers who were missing, and Jack thought, his heart sinking, "That must be one of them." Not wanting to frighten Kell, Jack rowed over to the object as casually as he could, and, sure enough, it was the body of a small boy. Jack lifted the victim into the boat.

"Come on, Kell," he ordered, through clenched teeth, "let's row for shore!"

As soon as they reached the beach, Jack told Kell, "Run up the beach and tell the lifeguard to get down here."

"Yes, Dad."

Kell dashed off as fast as his little legs could carry him. He was scared. He had never seen a dead person before. He felt sick in his stomach.

Finding the lifeguard, Kell stuttered, "T-t-there's a-a-a-" the words wouldn't come.

"Calm down, son," the lifeguard said. "Now tell me what's ailing you."

Kell took a deep breath and started over again.

"T-t-there's a-a kid . . . there's a kid down there. He's drowned, I think."

The lifeguard ran off to get an ambulance. Kell returned to his father. There was no hope for the victim. He had, in fact, been in the ocean for two or three days. He and his brother had been swimming, and they had gone out too far.

"See what happens when you get too fresh with the ocean," Jack said, turning to Kell. "They didn't respect the ocean."

Kell didn't go near the water again for two weeks. Better than a volume of words that experience had driven home his father's point.

When Kell wasn't rowing, he did pretty much the same things that most small boys like to do. He loved, for example, building model airplanes. Jack went up to Kell's room one afternoon and caught the boy bent over a drawing board. He had caught a bat, had it pinned to the board, and was tracing it.

"What are you doing, son?" Jack asked.

"Designing an airplane," Kell said. "Dad, why don't they build planes like birds—the way God did? If this bat can fly, then why can't planes be built like this to fly, too?"

Jack said he rightly didn't know the answer, but, in later years, he was to say to himself, "Darned if what Kell was talking about back there as a kid of eight wasn't similar to the design of today's jets—wings turned back, streamlined, etc. It's amazing a boy that age was so advanced in his thinking."

Kell always was a healthy lad, except when he was eleven years old and had scarlet fever. The doctor said no exercise, and Kell grew fat. His playmates teased him and called him Fatty. A year later, however, he had regained his health and was made coxswain of the Penn Athletic Club's intermediate eight-oared crew. Then, at thirteen, his Dad, who had never really pestered him much about rowing competitively, began urging him to row.

"Son," Jack would say, "you're not rowing enough. Better get out there on the river tomorrow."

Kell didn't like the idea much because the body contact sports had more appeal. He liked football, was a star at Penn Charter School in 1944.

"Son," Jack told him, "do you want to be just one of 200 best football players, or do you want to be the best in rowing? Get out there, boy, and put away those shoulder pads."

As Kell advanced in school, Jack would come home from the office and ask, "What did you do today, Kell?"

"I was fooling around with the weights in the gym."

"You're lazy. Quit wasting your time with those foolish things and get out your oars."

Kell finally confessed to himself, "I dread hearing that. I hate going out on the river. I don't love it anymore. The last thing I want to be is an oarsman." His father's relentless persistence actually was driving him away from what he, Jack, wanted most—a son who would be a champion sculler!

Then an important thing happened in the life and times of John Brendan Kelly, Jr. He was sent away to Pennsylvania Military Preparatory School when he was fourteen to correct his bad posture. He ate that military life up, making the riding team and boxing in the intramural tournament. He won an award for being a good cadet, but after two years the spark wore off and he welcomed returning to William Penn Charter School, a country day school in Philadelphia. Kell no longer resembled the pudgy youngster the kids in the Falls had called Fatty. The summers in the sun at Ocean City, the rigors of a life of discipline at military school, had developed that chunkiness into strong arms, chest and shoulders. It felt good to get back in a shell after two years.

The incident that clinched everything happened when Kell was fifteen years old. He was rowing on the river in a real shell for the first time, and it felt light and good, like changing from a plow horse to a thoroughbred. He was practicing with two other oarsmen. They had a sprint race, and, to the amazement of all, Kell won. He said to himself, "I know now this is my sport. I want to be the best sculler in the whole world."

That summer he teamed up with another lifeguard pal at Ocean City and won his first important race, beating men much older than himself. They were rowing a life boat, trailing most of the way, but at the last moment, by a stroke of luck, they caught a huge wave just right and rode it to victory. The sound of 10,000 spectators cheering sounded good to Kell's tender ears.

That night Jack was driving past the local Catholic church. There were two boys outside the door, apparently kneeling in prayer. "Do my eyes deceive me? Isn't that Kell?" Jack's eyes were telling the truth. It was Kell. He and his teammate had wanted to thank God for helping them win, and, finding the church doors closed, they simply knelt outside on the sidewalk and thanked Him from there.

The date of Kell's first big victory, incidentally, was Friday, the 13th! He was later to discover that the girl who was to become his wife, Mary Freeman, won her first National Senior backstroke and medley swimming championship—on April the *13th,* 1951.

After his Ocean City triumph, Kell began a ceaseless campaign to capture the Diamond Sculls for the Kellys.

"That's the one your Dad wants, Kell," his mother told him. "He's had his heart set on you winning it almost from the day you were born. He doesn't talk much about it, but it's there."

Kell won the National Schoolboy single sculls championship in 1944, and the following year in the Peoples Regatta, on July 4th, he really cut loose and won five championships —in one afternoon, a world's record. His Dad once won four titles in a single day, but never five. Kell was only eighteen at the time, it was his first open regatta, yet he bagged the junior single title, intermediate single, association single, senior single, and senior one-fourth mile dash. It is never likely to happen again. In 1945, he also won the Canadian Schoolboy and Senior titles before going into the Navy.

All the time Kell was rowing he was also boxing. When he was sixteen, his father had sent him to Al Nino, trainer and athletic director at one of the clubs in Philadelphia.

"Toughen the boy up," Jack told Al. "Make a man out of him."

"Will do," Nino said.

Al figured to put the pressure on the boy immediately. There would be no messing around.

"Come on, kid, put these on." He handed Kell a pair of boxing gloves. Kell said nothing, following instructions.

Al thought, "I'll find out right off how much guts this kid has. No doubt he's a typical rich kid. I won't pull my punches." Nino shot the works. He hit Kell with everything but the ring posts. Kell didn't take a backward step, and, head down, he kept plowing in, giving it as well as taking it. He took quite a thrashing.

Finally, Nino said, "That's all for today. Go take a shower." And, to himself, Al muttered, "He will be like all the others and never come back." But Kell did come back, again and again. And he kept coming back. For three months Nino boxed his ears. After each session both were puffy-lipped and bleeding. Not once did Kell say anything.

At last, Al said, "I take it all back, kid. When you first came to me I thought you were like all the rest of these rich kids. You're not. You have it here"—he pressed his finger against his heart—"you're all thoroughbred." Jack also had Tommy O'Keefe, a good lightweight fighter, teach Kell the fine points of the game.

In 1945, when Kell went into the Navy as an apprentice seaman, teaching whaleboat rowing to other gobs, he won the heavyweight boxing championship of his regiment at Bainbridge. The young man had learned his lessons well.

Jack was fifty-five when he challenged Kell, then seventeen, to an eighth-of-a-mile race on the Schuylkill. Since he knew much more about racing than his son, Jack brazenly stole the start on the boy. Try as Kell did, he just couldn't catch his Dad.

"I will never race you again," Jack said, after the race. And to a friend later, he grinned, "I guess you can say I retired undefeated."

"Hale America"

Jack and Margaret Kelly never have claimed to be model parents, but in bringing up their own four children they put just as much emphasis on their physical as on their mental and moral development. While they were still babies, Jack would hoist them high in the air when they clutched his fingers. This pulling and stretching strengthened their muscles.

As the youngsters grew older, their parents took them on regular outings to the beach and elsewhere and encouraged them to play strenuous games. Later, they installed a small gym on the third floor of their home, with a punching bag, weights, a rowing machine, and other athletic equipment. And they insisted that the children use it regularly.

In 1938, Jack began to realize with grave alarm how few American children were getting the same physical fitness training. And with Hitler on the march in Europe, and trouble brewing in the Orient, the picture was all the more frightening.

Bleakly, he said to his wife one evening, "Margaret, there's going to be another war, sure as shootin'. Those war clouds are beginning to blow like locusts in our direction, and the United States isn't physically prepared for trouble. We're a bunch of panty-waists. The President ought to be told of the facts."

The "facts" were these: the United States prided itself on being a nation of he-men, a vast physical blend of Atlas, Dempsey and Gargantua. We could whip the whey out of anybody in the house. If you wanted to bet, we could do it with one hand tied behind our back. But now came the disillusionment. Kelly, who had done some intricate study on the subject, had reason to believe that thirty-three per cent of the flower of our young manhood were physically unfit to wear a military uniform. The figures were appalling.

Coincidentally, President Roosevelt was making a major political speech at a Democratic rally in Philadelphia that night, and Jack was scheduled to introduce him to the gathering. Since they would be seated together on the dais, Kelly figured to tell the chief executive of his survey.

Jack didn't mess around. He got right to the point the moment they put their heads together.

"Let's face fundamentals," Jack said bluntly. "We are supposed to be the most sports-minded country in the world. Our yearly bills for sports equipment and sports admissions reach astronomical figures. We play as hard as we work—maybe harder—and yet I will predict if ever we have a draft thirty-three per cent of our men will fail the physical examinations."

Jack's remarks caught the President off balance, staggering him a little.

"Nonsense," FDR said, "it won't be that bad. Aren't you exaggerating a little?"

"I wish you were right," said Jack.

It is not easy to be proven wrong in a serious matter, and the President added, "The figure will be closer to twenty-five per cent."

The tiny seed planted by Kelly in 1938 began to germinate when the draft became law. About a month or two after our young men started to have their corpuscles examined Jack received a wire from the President.

"You win," he wired. "Figures startling. Forty-five per cent are rejects. Must do something. Come to Washington as soon as possible."

Scenting serious trouble if things continued at such a rate, Jack hastily flew to Washington at the President's invitation. This time his words fell upon receptive ears. The President looked troubled. A new air of decision had settled on him.

"The country needs looking into—right away," FDR said movingly. "Many of our recruits are as flabby and fragile as you told me three years ago. What are your ideas?"

"A physical fitness program."

"Will you direct it?"

"Yes."

"Then by Presidential decree, I appoint you Federal Director of Physical Fitness."

After the meeting things really got going. Kelly had a big and important job on his hands, the biggest of his life, and he knew it. The non-salaried post didn't make for exciting reading, and it wasn't exciting in the doing, but the old world's champion sculler went to town on it in his usual vigorous manner.

At first sight the President couldn't have picked a better man than Kelly to go to work and do a Paul Revere on the nation's dormant muscles. At fifty-three, Jack was in his full florescence—a handsome man, his face ruddy with good living, tall and as straight up and down as six o'clock, with eager eyes and a sprinkling of gray hair, whose roots were firmly implanted in the fertile soil of the American sports, political and business oasis.

Jack kept himself in shape. Every morning for a good many years he continued to labor away on the oars. It wasn't easy. There were mornings when he'd rather lie in bed. He did lie there some mornings, trying to make up excuses for not going out on the river. But he always wound up by going because he knew that if he quit for one day, he'd quit for good. Even today his form has remained trim and hard. He has put on very few pounds. He tells his tailor to make his clothes just as he always has made them. Then he has to stay fit so he can wear them.

One of Jack's slogans as high priest of the nation's physical conditioning program was "Hale America!" and another was "It's Fun To Be Fit." The wealth of a nation is in the strength of its people. If anybody could have thought of better ones, Kelly would have snatched at them with glee.

There wasn't a single thing that could be said against Jack's movement and many things that could be said in favor of it—and Kelly said those things with gusto. The only trouble was getting people to listen, or to take action after listening. The public did not realize it, but we were getting closer and closer to regimentation in many ways. Happily Jack's National Health program had its virtues and did not conflict with any of the four freedoms. Nobody objected seriously to a move designed to add to his physical solvency.

The public was indifferent to Kelly's program at first. The story of fatalities from ticker trouble had been spread so often guys were scared to death to scratch themselves energetically for fear of unduly straining their hearts and dropping dead on the spot.

"In case of war," Jack told one group, "we'll walk, not run, to the nearest bomb shelter for the simple reason that the 100-yard dash probably will do more damage than bombs to most of us. Despite all the propaganda to the contrary, we're getting fatter and flabbier. The average American male, who resembles anything but a Greek god on the loose, settles his lap on his knees, moves as close as he can get to his desk, and nature continues its disintegrating course. Nothing can frighten him, apparently, into getting into shape except the far-fetched prospect of having some sinuous siren appraise his physique and register judgment in a glance that plainly means 'fat slob,' or 'skinny punk.' "

Jack took lots of good-natured kidding about his physical fitness program, but he didn't mind. He was at Harrisburg, Pennsylvania, one evening talking to some educators. Among other things he told them was that our educational program was lopsided. It gave too much attention to the mind and not enough to the body. Jack said to them:

"I have four children and I see them coming home every night with their arms filled with books and sit down to two and a half hours of home work. I believe in educating a child, of course. But I don't believe in piling it on them like that and, in some cases, making nervous wrecks of them. I would prefer to see them have more time for games and sports."

Kelly could see that some of his listeners didn't like what he was saying. The next day one of the local Harrisburg newspapers had a headline over the story of the meeting:

"Kelly Wants Them Dumber and Stronger."

Jack said, "Well, all right. That would suit me. I had to work for my education. I went to night school. I studied hard. But I studied the things I wanted to learn and that would be useful to me—and still managed to find time for sport."

Another night he was talking to a group of middle-aged men, telling them what his program was trying to do. "I was also trying to show them how they could improve their physical condition," Jack said. "When I was through, one comfortably upholstered gent glared at me and said, 'Do you know what you are? You are nothing but an over-age destroyer!'"

Jack's plan was to get everybody exercising, and he meant everybody! He even figured out special exercises for office men who had to bend over a hot desk all day working on defense plans. He had another special set of exercises for housewives whose muscles were tied into bow knots bending over washtubs all day, or wielding brooms.

"Nothing like it," Jack said, "to make them supple and strong and ready for another day's washing."

When Bob Considine got wind of Kelly's plans to help grandmaw pour herself back into a size ten, he flexed his muscles, did a couple of knee bends, sucked in his stomach and thrust out his chest instead of vice versa, and told his readers:

"Will you please stop reading this article, slip on a sweater, and trot four quick laps around the block? How about getting up an hour earlier all next week and exercising? Next time you drive some place, why not park the bus a half mile from your destination, and walk the rest of the way?"

By the time his readers had finished galumphing through that first paragraph, they were so exhausted they reminded one of birds heavy with sedatives.

"Kelly's got a big job, getting blubbery old Pop to do something about that bay window," Considine said. "Mom, herself, might be a whisper easier to move, however. She's always yapping about going on that radish juice and stewed fern diet and taking up golf or handstands, so she can trust a fast glance at the mirror. So get out of those chairs, y'bums!"

One of Considine's colleagues, Henry McLemore, was not quite so enthusiastic. The thought of going to a gym and working up a sweat so that he smelled like a stevedore horrified him. Exercise was a ghastly word.

"Jeez," gasped McLemore, "Jack Kelly is busily rounding

up a staff of great athletes to see that every man, woman and child play at games. How much better it would have been to select instructors in the same condition as their pupils—spindly shanks, curvature of the belly, etcetera. The very sight of them gives you an inferiority complex. It would be fun just once to be led in calisthenics by a skinny, rundown gent who admitted at the start of the class that he wasn't too sure if he could bend over without falling on his face, and that for everyone to keep his street clothes on because he, the instructor, looked like a scarecrow in a gym suit."

Despite the ribbing, Kelly and his assistants kept after the sit-down strikers and made it so hot for them that at least a lot of them got up and took a walk, if only to get away from Jack and his men.

After the United States got in the war, Americans began to take Kelly's program seriously. There was no fooling around now. The enemy meant business. Jack stressed mass civilian physical training as a preparedness measure in his lectures. He cited Japanese swimmers as Grade A examples of the value and results of fitness programs.

"The Japanese swimmers looked ridiculous in the 1924 Olympic Games," he told one civilian group, "yet I could see they were trying. They went back to Japan and practiced. In the 1932 Olympics they won most of the important places. Then, suddenly, we all read how they swam with full packs for a mile or so in the assault on Hongkong. How many of our own troops could do that before World War II? Not many. We've got to keep fit, for in time of war it's a civilian battle as much as it's a soldier's fight. I remember the old English woman who was dug out of the ruins of her home, after a severe bombing. When the air raid wardens asked, 'Is your husband still under the debris?' she replied, 'No, he's in the army—the bloody coward!' "

Kelly was telling a friend about his physical fitness program recently and what was wrong with the country's health in general.

"Too many escalators, elevators and automobiles," Jack snorted. "Everybody rides. If they're not riding they are sitting. We just sit and sit and sit. We start our sitting at a very tender age. Our young people get off to a bad start. They are pampered and petted. Our young men are too much concerned with good times, and not enough concerned about their fundamental job of being men. Most of our youngsters don't want to work, and will not work when given the opportunity. Instead of continuing to spoil them, we should be teaching them that the world doesn't owe them a living. They should be taught that they have to hustle.

"Judging from the impressive records of U.S. athletes, we are inclined to feel that everybody in America is in top physical condition. That is wrong. Dr. Hans Kraus of New York University recently made a serious study to prove the point. His survey took a number of kids, aged six to sixteen, in this country and compared their muscular fitness with a similar group in Austria, Italy and Switzerland. He gave them six simple exercises, such as bending over and touching the floor with their finger tips without bending their knees. The report shows that 57.9 per cent of American youngsters failed in one or more of the six tests, whereas only 8.9 per cent of the European children failed them. In other words, almost six out of ten of our children were found physically unfit compared to less than one out of ten in the three European countries.

"In an effort to do something about this danger, I instigated a White House luncheon in the Summer of 1955, at which President Eisenhower was given Dr. Kraus' report. The President was shocked. He said the situation was more serious than he had imagined and slated a national conference to deal with it."

Jack has always practiced what he preaches. One morning he walked into Philadelphia's Pennsylvania Station. There is an escalator in the depot which folks were *waiting* to get on. Right next to the escalator is a stairway, and not a soul was using it.

"Do you think those people waiting in line to get on the escalator would take the trouble to walk up and down the stairs?" asked Jack. "Not on your life!"

"Did you use the stairs?" Jack was asked.

"Of course," he replied. "You don't think I'd take the escalator and knock my own campaign, do you?"

Bringing Up The Kellys

During the World War II years, as her children continued to develop into robust, lively children, Margaret Kelly showed that the old-fashioned virtues were still intact. To teach them discipline and respect for their elders, she was often strict with Peggy, Kell, Grace and Lizanne, even severe when she had to be, but always fair and understanding.

Religion, naturally, figured importantly in their training. Before beginning each meal, the youngsters collaborated in saying a little prayer. The dialogue went like this:

Peggy: Bless us, Oh Lord, and these thy gifts we are about to receive from thy bounty through Christ our Lord.

Kell: Do unto others as you would have others do unto you.

Grace: Politeness is to do and say the kindest thing in the kindest way.

Lizanne: Amen.

The Kelly home, across the Schuylkill from the Main Line, was the meeting place for the whole neighborhood. There was a lawn out back with swings, a sandbox, tennis court, and whatnot. Summers, the family went to Ocean City on the Jersey shore.

Of the three Kelly girls, Peggy was the gay one, the pixie. Lizanne was an extrovert and independent. Grace was somewhat shy and quiet, sempiternally annoyed by a chronic head cold. Her parents seriously considered taking her to Arizona, a drier and hotter climate.

Kell rated his sisters superior type females—i.e., as long as they stayed away from the "Tomato Men," a neighborhood club he had organized. As leader, Kell built a clubhouse in the Kellys' backyard, and promptly told Grace and Lizanne to stay out. Peggy was granted visiting privileges, however. She could pin all the boys in the neighborhood!

Grace and Lizanne and their girl friends started a club of their own. They built a doll house at the opposite end of the backyard and tacked a "No Boys Allowed" sign over the door.

One morning Mrs. Kelly, who was busy in the basement, heard a lot of noise coming from the backyard. Peeking her head out to investigate, there were the girls peppering the boys' clubhouse with tomatoes from the family's Victory Garden. Both sides, boys and girls, dripped tomato juice from head to foot. The Victory Garden was virtually demolished. And when Mrs. Kelly had finished reading the riot act, that was the end of the "Tomato Men" and doll house.

Peggy was no longer the tomboy by the time a handsome young man named George Davis popped into her life. They met at Ocean City. She was a pretty young thing, with eyes of blue and silky blond hair. George had been an All-American soccer player at the University of Pennsylvania. He was by now an Ensign in the Navy.

Mrs. Kelly is a modern mother with old-fashioned ideas

about raising children, and she illustrated this one night down at the beach house when Peggy made a date to go out with George.

The Kellys were having dinner guests, and after eating, Peggy excused herself from the table and hurried up to her room. An hour later she reappeared looking like a Vogue cover girl. George was waiting for her out on the sun porch. Peggy started for the door.

"Where are you going, young lady?" her mother called out.

"I have a date with George, mother," said Peggy.

"Well, George will have to wait," Mrs. Kelly said. "It's your turn on the dishes tonight."

Peggy washed and George wiped.

Because of the war, George and Peggy decided to get married in a hurry. Neither wanted a long engagement, so within a short time they were rushing around completing arrangements, getting Peggy's clothes together and so forth. The family worked hard and quickly. The wedding day, in 1944, came, and it went off beautifully. The wedding banquet was over, everybody was dancing at the reception and enjoying themselves tremendously.

Grace, Lizanne and their mother happened to be standing together, and they saw Kell and his father with their heads together off in another corner of the room. The men saw them and came over.

"Come on, girls, it's getting late," Jack said. "We have to get home. Kell has a race coming up next week."

It was only eleven o'clock and the Kelly women were really having a fine time.

Young Lizanne was only nine years old, but she piped up: "Listen, dad, we want to stay and dance. You get your car and pack up your prize pup and take him home and put him to bed."

Kell was known as the family's prize pup after that.

While her brother rowed, Grace, then eleven, spent much of her time at the Old Academy Players, a Philadelphia playhouse where Peggy also had been active. She got her first part in "The Women," and was very proud of herself the night she came home and told the others about it. Nobody worked harder than the little Kelly girl during rehearsals.

Two days before the opening, Grace sat with the family eating dinner. Dress rehearsal was being held that night. Grace was so excited she could hardly eat.

"Grace," spoke her mother, shaking her back to earth, "what are those spots on your face?"

Grace rubbed her hand across her face.

"I don't know, mother," she replied.

"Come here," commanded her mother. Mrs. Kelly took a closer look at Grace's face. "Why . . . off to bed, young lady! You've caught the measles."

"But, mother, I'm supposed to be at rehearsal in an hour," protested Grace.

"Can't be helped," said Mrs. Kelly. "You've got the measles. Peggy can take your place."

Mrs. Kelly turned to Peggy (this incident was a couple of years before Peggy's marriage) and said, "You will have to go and fill in for Gracie."

"But, mother," said Peggy, "I don't know the part."

"Then you will have to learn it," said Mrs. Kelly.

"Yes, mother," said Peggy.

Peggy rushed over to rehearsal that evening, explained her younger sister's plight. She studied Grace's role while being made up and most of that night. The following evening she gave a flawless performance.

Grace became a fixture at the Old Academy Players during her girlhood. When she wasn't there, or at school, she was usually at home, absorbed in books. She also wrote poetry, some serious, some "little gooney ones" that showed a neat turn of phrase. Sample: "I hate to see the sun go down . . . And squeeze itself into the ground . . . Since some warm night it might get stuck . . . And in the morning not get up."

But from the time she was six years old and performing minor parts in home theatricals ("Somebody always got the lead") organized by Peggy, Grace wanted only to be on the stage.

Meanwhile, the war in Europe and the South Pacific raged on. The headlines of the day were dreary and took most of the fun out of being young. Youngsters grew up awfully fast.

Kell was a lad of only fourteen when he said to Jack: "Dad, you told me that you fought in the First World War, a war to save the world for democracy. You told me we won that war. So why all this fighting now?"

Jack probed deeply into his conscience. What could he say? He couldn't find an answer, but later, after considerable thought, Jack wrote his son a letter. He felt he owed it to Kell to put his answer on record. Later, in a nation-wide radio broadcast over the CBS network, Jack read the letter to millions.

"I'm not going to pull any punches on my generation," wrote Jack. "You have a right to ask such a question. It is embarrassing, but your generation has a right to the truth.

"Son, we did win the war, or we thought we won it, but when we sat around the table at Versailles, everybody wanted to cut the pie. We didn't think in terms of projecting peace over the years without bitterness, without revenge. We were concerned only with what was immediately best for us, or with getting even with someone.

"President Woodrow Wilson proposed a League of Nations, but our Congressmen, with an eye to expediency rather than patriotism or humanity, made an issue of it with the result that it failed. Right now a number of our Congressmen and Senators are looking at November rather than the Philippines. President Wilson's plan may not have been a perfect solution but at least it was designed to make the world a better place in which to live. I am certain if the United States had taken an active part in the League something would have evolved from our participation that might have prevented the chaos of today.

"Then in the Roaring Twenties, when we made money our God instead of thinking of the God and his teaching that we learned at our mothers' knees, we forgot all about the Golden Rule. Our one idea was to outsmart each other. We substituted cleverness for honesty. We made new rules for the game. You don't remember the stock market boom and the land booms in Florida. Well, son, it was the feast of Belshazzar.

"When you deal in excesses, son, somebody has to pay. When you don't think in terms of decency and honesty and charity, then some God's law makes you pay.

"Our bankers and the French and English bankers supplied the money to Japan and Germany to build the war machinery they are using against us now. Even up until 1940 we were selling Japan all its gasoline and scrap iron. Now we are paying in blood and tears for the thirty pieces of silver that we took in profit.

"Pearl Harbor was a rude awakening but somehow or other, my philosophy of life is, 'Whatever is is best.' If that had not occurred to jolt us out of our lethargy, the increasing division of our country might have led us to a worse fate. Labor and Capital were at each other's throat. Strikes were multiplying all over the country with bloodshed at many of the plants. That could not continue. If that little yellow man who won't be there when this is over did one thing, he gave us unity and made us realize how much we need each other in dark hours.

"We needed a lesson and we needed a chastening, which we are now getting. We cannot think in any terms but that we will win the war and now is the time to take stock of ourselves. We weren't wholly bad. We were not aggressors, but we were careless. We didn't appreciate the fact that we can read any newspaper and any magazine or any news without restriction that is printed. We can turn on the radio and listen to any station in the world. We can go to our polling places to cast our vote and there is no Stormtrooper looking over our shoulder and telling us we must vote 'ja. We didn't stand erect when the Star Spangled Banner was played and look up to Heaven and thank God that we live in a free land. We used to move about during the playing of our National Anthem and just accepted our flag and Anthem as our rightful heritage. We thought we were born to the purple. We didn't think that we had to pay for that privilege. So we had a lesson coming to us.

"But your generation, Kell, better known as the youth, has much to learn. The things that I am going to say do not necessarily mean you, because you have been better than the average, but I am fearful of the fourteen to eighteen year old period, the know-it-all years.

"Many of you don't appreciate the blessings that you have. Many of you leave much to be desired in manners. You don't give to your elders the respect that you should. Every one of you is going to school; some one is making a sacrifice for each one of you so that you may live as well as you do. Yet your attitude is that you are doing your parents a favor by going to school and learning to cope with the problems you will have to face.

"You start to your dances at eleven o'clock at night. You don't seem to think you are having a good time unless it is on night shift. Many of you smoke and drink at fifteen and are too sophisticated generally. You have had the advantage of movies and newspapers and magazines and compulsory education up to eighteen years of age, and all of this, instead of making you grateful, has made you blasé. Now you have a direct challenge from the youth of Germany and Japan and Italy. I feel sure you will measure up. But you can't meet them on equal grounds unless you prepare and that is what I am trying to get across to you. I think all you need is just a little awakening exactly as we did. You all have the right stuff in you and I have a great deal of confidence in you. Perhaps it is our fault. We have failed to discipline you. But despite whose fault it is, the deed is done.

"I have confessed the shortcomings of my generation to you, son, and I have told you a few of the things I see wrong about yours. You have been better than the average and I wouldn't trade you if I could. But I will soon have to toss the torch to you to carry aloft. The torch is liberty, the greatest and most valuable thing I can give you, so guard it well. If any one tries to take it away from you, I would rather see you die defending it than live and surrender it. Just remember that Colin Kelly of our clan had that same decision to make recently in the South Pacific.

"And, Kell, if that privilege ever comes to you, I hope you acquit yourself as well."

In 1945, Kell, along with thousands of other American athletes, served a hitch in the Navy. It may have been the end of sculling for him because, what with one thing and another, he may have lost interest in the sport, or the Navy may have had other notions about his future. It could have been a couple of years at least before he found out which way he was going.

For some athletes, it was the end, but Kell got a break. The Navy, recognizing that a champion in its ranks is good for purposes of recruitment, told the nineteen year old seaman to go on with his rowing.

So Kell rowed—and how.

The war was over when the Philadelphia sports writers officially requested the Navy to transfer Kell to duty in England. Coincidentally the transfer came through only a few weeks before the Diamond Sculls. Here, at last, a Kelly was going to row at Henley. Despite the fact he had captured both North American titles, Kell had very little time to get back into rowing shape after his absence from regular competition.

No doubt the boys who write fiction could have given the story a happier finish. Certainly all of the elements were there. But life is not the work of a master dramatist. The hero does not always appear out of a cloud of fire at the supreme moment, slay the bad dragon, and then vanish again. No, life creates its own scenario. We are only the characters.

In the first heat, July 3, Kell beat an Englishman named J. H. Pinches. He met another Englishman the following afternoon, and this being the anniversary of the Declaration of Independence, Kell made it two straight. The scoreboard read: Kell 2, England 0. In the semi-finals, he drew Art Gallagher, a former national champion and a fellow Philadelphian, beating him in a grueling race for his nineteenth straight victory. Now he was in the finals and the pressure was mounting. Stories of how his father was rejected in 1920 by Henley stewards filled papers all over the world. Kell was exhausted. He did his best, but it wasn't quite enough. The terrible strain of three straight days of racing had left Kell limp. He had melted off ten pounds, his stamina was spent. He lost by three lengths to Jean Sephariades, a Frenchman, after being even with him until the last quarter.

"Never mind, son," consoled his father, who had watched the championship race from a launch. "You knocked the British out, didn't you? It has been a long time, but a Kelly finally did it. This isn't the end. You're coming back again and again until the name of Kelly is inscribed on the Diamond Sculls."

Jack turned to a reporter and said, "Ever notice how much Kell's hands are like mine?" He held out his sturdy paws, now free from the marks of hard labor. "The boy can work with them, too."

While all of the Kellys took the defeat in stride, Mike Murphy, a wealthy Philadelphia rowing fan, screamed bloody murder. Claiming Kell had been done an injustice, he cried, "The luck of the draw favored the Frenchman. He had practically no opposition in the preliminary heats, while Kell had to meet the very best and was completely exhausted by the time he got to the finals."

Murphy offered to put up $5000 for Sephariades to come to Philadelphia and race Kell on the Schuylkill the following Labor Day. When Jack heard about the offer, he exploded.

"Let the Frenchman rest on his laurels," he said. "He beat Kell fairly. He's the champ."

But as Jack said it, he was already making plans for next year.

Poetic Justice

Back at Henley again. A year has passed since Kell lost to the Frenchman. He has completed his hitch in the Navy and has returned to his studies at the University of Pennsylvania. There have been few idle moments, for in between classwork Kell has been out on the river diligently preparing himself for another crack at the coveted Diamond Sculls. Now the hour has arrived.

It's a bright, warm July afternoon. More than 40,000 gaily-clad Britishers mill about, oblivious to the tall, straight, middle-aged American standing off alone on the banks of the Thames. He appears strangely out of place. If passers-by had taken the time to study him, they would have seen that he would have been far more at home out on the river, crouched in the frail shell of a boat, oars flashing in the powerful rhythmic beat that had made him the most feared, far and away the most famous of all oarsmen. None in that crowd recognized Jack Kelly.

Twenty-seven years ago he had been world's champion. Now here he stood, alone with his memories. True, he had evened the score with John Bull in the 1920 Olympic Games, but his great triumph had lost some of its punch with the bitter memory of the humiliating rejection that still rankled in his mind.

So this was D-Day! D for Diamond Sculls.

Kell's defeat on this same racing course in 1946 had not discouraged them. Whenever the boy's spirits drooped, Jack quoted a line from grandmother Kelly: "A licking is not a failure. You are never done, unless you let yourself stay licked." Kell had not yet been born when grandmother Kelly passed on, but not a day went by that he did not hear his father speak of her. She must have been an amazing person, he thought.

Once, when Jack lost a big race, she had wired him:

"How many times did Caesar flunk?
How many times was Nelson sunk?"

Jack had watched his son stroke his way past one oarsman after another to reach this day, the Diamond Sculls finals. Only a few moments ago Jack had stood at the dock and wished Kell the best of luck. The scene came back to him:

Kell, fitting himself in his shell, had lifted his gaze to meet his father's eyes.

"I will do my best, dad," said Kell.

"This is the one we have waited for, son," said Jack. "The past doesn't count now. All of our previous wins have only been a build-up to this moment."

Jack grabbed Kell's hand and squeezed it. Then he dipped down for a handful of water and baptized the boy, a ritual they repeated before every race. Jack straightened up.

"Well, let's go," he said clearly. To say any more would be to betray his feelings in the words trembling on his tongue.

Kell looked up at his dad and said, "I will meet you here at the dock after the race." Shoving off, he paddled slowly toward the starting line up the river.

"Good luck, son," Jack called after him.

Around Jack, now, the murmur of the crowd's excitement and air of anticipation was, even after all these years, still a fresh and wonderful thing to hear. He had rowed innumerable times and heard that sound, before many of the people around him were even born, and yet it remained the same through two world wars and changing generations, a true essence and trademark of sport.

Glancing around him, Jack's eyes were caught and held by the heterogeneous selection of bright colors the spectators were wearing. The scene was tuppence-colored to an incredibly un-English extent, all shades of greens, reds, blues and the olive green of the trees. It was the most hat-conscious crowd he had ever seen, young men, middle-aged gents, old codgers wearing little blue and white caps, pink caps, red and blue caps, tartan caps, and straw hats. There were flashing blazers, club ties, braces, the famous Leander socks, and old gentlemen who had not rowed for a half-century were cut out in their Nineteenth Century best. Against the green of the willow banks it was the men, as tradition demanded, who were really outstyling the ladies. The colored caps and socks, boaters, striped flannels and blazers reminded Jack of a happy collection of overgrown Billie Bunters and benevolent Aubrey Smiths. More near-millionaires than watermen were dotting this stretch of the Thames, and Jack thought to himself, "This is a social production, as well as a sports event, worthy of DeMille."

All the years, Jack thought, all the oarsmen and people he had known through the years; many were gone now, but he was here, one middle-aged man with a dream in his heart and the decision just minutes away. Jack had wanted the Diamond Sculls trophy so long that even now it was difficult to realize that at last the fulfilment of his dream was in sight.

Countless stories, amounting to almost a legend, had been written about how Jack had been denied the right to compete on this same course twenty-seven years before, and vowed that a day would come when he would come over with a son—"a gentleman and a scholar! and a sculler as well"—and win it. Jack's heart skipped a beat as his eyes focused on Kell gliding up the river toward something the writers liked to term a date with destiny. What must be going through his son's mind this very second?

Reaching the starting line, a quiet excitement welled up inside Kell as he jockeyed his boat into position. He glanced across at his opponent, Carl Fronsdal of Norway, who had also streaked through all of his heats. Kell thought, "This is your day, Kell. You've got to win. Everybody back in America is counting on you. And you have to win it for dad and the family."

A wave of confidence swept over him. Down deep he felt he couldn't lose. He was at his peak, despite four days of rugged rowing. He had sailed right through the preliminary heats, winning by wide margins. He had beaten Piesseus of Belgium by four lengths in the first heat, then Habbits of England easily, and Bushnell of England by four lengths in the third heat. His times had been much faster than the Norwegian's, so why shouldn't he win? Now an inner warmth filled him as he remembered saying goodby to his mother and Grace and Lizanne back at the hotel a few hours earlier. They were sitting out there some place in the swirling sea of faces. His dad was not with them, as he had wanted to watch the race from another vantage point. Peggy wasn't there at all. She was back in the States with her husband, George Davis. Mrs. Kelly had made the sign of the Cross on Kell's back with her forefinger—exactly like grandmother Kelly used to do with his dad before each race —and said affectionately, "God speed, son."

Back on shore, Jack waited patiently, the hope and dream of long years coming up thick and strong and living in his throat. The old excitement was still strangely there. A feeling seemed to be crying aloud in his chest—"Somehow it has to be."

Jack was abruptly jerked out of his daydream by a tumultuous roar.

"They're off!"

Jack couldn't see Kell explode to the front as if propelled by a gun, but fortunately for his state of mind, he could hear an account of the start via the loud speaker.

Jack stood a mile and a half away from the starting line as he had wanted to see the finish. Every quarter of a mile the loud speaker announcer gave the position of the scullers.

Kell, wearing a replica of the Kelly-green hat his dad had worn in the 1920 Olympics, quickly settled down to a steady, rhythmic beat. Stroke . . . stroke . . . stroke! Kell was rowing beautifully. And, stroke by stroke, rhythmically, powerfully, Jack was rowing every beat of the way with his son.

Passing the half-way post, Kell had increased his lead to three lengths over the Norwegian. He saw Fronsdal trying desperately to gain water, then start to fade back. Kell told himself: "Now is the time to pour it on. Take what heart he has left out of him."

Kell tightened his grip. His oars flashed and ripped with a swirl through the water and spray. The tremendous pace was starting to tell on him, too. His eyes stung with sweat. He fought hard to get his breath. His tongue tasted like a dry bone, his back ached, and his arms began to grow weary. But he couldn't quit.

And now, as Kell hit the last half mile, Jack's field glasses brought the tense drama home to him. The uncertainty of the public address system's reports had been maddening, even if Kell was in the lead.

Silently, Jack prayed his son could hold on. "Please, God, no hard luck, no tough breaks, as long as the boy is proving the better sculler. Don't let him break an oar, 'catch a crab' —or fall overboard."

Kell bent grimly to his task. Down the last hundred yards he felt that he was rowing on nerve alone. Yet, as Jack saw from shore, Kell was actually extending his lead over the Norwegian. Four lengths . . . five lengths . . . now six! Kell obviously was guarding against any desperate last-second sprint by his opponent.

All the way down that last stretch, Kell kept muttering, "For you, dad, this one's for you."

Above the tumult and the shouting, Kell could hear the loud, clear voice of an Englishman:

"Well sculled, Kelly!"

Now Kell put all the heart and strength he could muster into those last ten strokes. Pull . . . tug . . . grip. "For you, dad, this one's for you." There was a tinge of wild jubilance within him, replacing the grim, determined expression he had worn on his face all the way down the river. Three more strokes . . . two more strokes . . . one more!

Kell sat hunched over in his boat, regaining his breath and energy. He had an eight length lead when he glided across the finish line. The final chapter of the Kelly versus

Diamond Sculls saga had been written. With the cheers of thousands crashing down on him, Kell gripped his oars and slowly rowed over to the press stand to congratulate and pose with Fronsdal for the photographers, and to receive formal congratulations. But, above all, to receive the Diamond Sculls trophy from Lady Hambelton, a lady-in-waiting to the Queen.

Through the ceremony Kell kept searching the crowd for his dad. Oh, there he was, waiting back at the dock. Kell's heart jumped wildly. Right now he wanted to be with his father more than anything. Excusing himself, he slipped back into his boat, and paddled to the dock in record time.

"Well, dad, we did it!" he shouted. Not "I" did it, but "we" did it. Jack had been waiting for this moment so long that his body suddenly felt odd and faraway. Emotion contorted his face. Tears trickled down his cheeks. It was a moment rich in drama as father and son hugged each other.

Up in the press coop, writers from every country sat down to invest the event with epic grandeur. For some, the story flowed as fluently as the Kelly tears. For others, the words would not come.

One American correspondent, who had been close to the Kelly story and knew what the son's victory meant to the father, sat motionless at his typewriter and stared blankly into space. Then he got up and began pacing back and forth, looking morose. A colleague, who had already completed his own deathless prose, asked him what was the matter. The frustrated correspondent cussed himself roundly.

"Darnit!" he barked, "I've been waiting for this to happen for years, and now that it's happened I can't write it."

While Kell showered, a reporter interviewed Jack, who by this time had recovered his composure.

"Well, you Kellys finally won the big one," said the newspaperman.

"Yes," smiled Jack, "it is like a dream. I've waited twenty-seven years for this moment."

The reporter said, "I guess every father who loves his son, and in turn is fortunate enough to have the boy's affection, dreams of a moment like this, and its wallop."

"It's something like Sorrel and Son, an old story, but true," replied Jack gravely. "When it finally came to me today, there weren't any words that could do justice to my feelings, and there aren't any now."

"In your imagination," said the reporter, "I suppose you thought of how you would gloat when this day came."

"I felt that way at times," confessed Jack. "But now that it's here all I have is a tremendous feeling of pride for Kell. He's the one that matters, not the thwarted ambition of an old guy who once got his fingers publicly slapped over here because he was born without a silver spoon in his mouth."

"Mr. Kelly," said the reporter, "what your boy did this afternoon is a definite victory over snobbery." The reporter paused, then asked, "Was that little green hat your son wore today the same one that you used to wear when you raced?"

Jack shook his head.

"No," he said, "but it was a replica of the one I wore when I won the 1920 Olympic championship at Antwerp. It was another symbol, of course. I wanted something of mine to ride across the Henley finish line today to make up for the heartbreak I suffered in 1920."

Jack was silent for a moment, then added, "But I know now that the replica of the green cap wasn't the slightest importance at the showdown. That was my son out there—to me the greatest singles sculler that ever lived.

"For all of me," said Jack, tapping his chest with a forefinger, "he couldn't have changed that if he had worn a beret!"

Peggy, Grace, baby Lizanne, Kell and mother smile charmingly for photographer.

Jack, Sr. twirls Grace on the sands at Ocean City.

Always a close family, Jack, Sr., Grace, Lizanne, Margaret and Kell pause here between play for the camera.

Grace Kelly—stars in her eyes.

A pair of budding shamrocks, Grace, left, and sister Lizanne.

The John B. Kellys and children from the 1935 family album.

The Kellys at home.

The Kelly women, looking like budding shamrocks, go shopping.

Jack, Sr. and daughters work in Victory Garden at home during World War II. Left to right, Peggy, Lizanne and Grace.

The Kelly kids during their teenage years: Lizanne, left, Grace, Peggy, and Kell.

Another group photo from the family album, taken at their Ocean City, New Jersey, summer place.

Mr. and Mrs. John B. Kelly toast each other on twenty-fifth wedding anniversary in Philadelphia. Grace, left, George Davis (Peggy's husband), Peggy, Kell and Lizanne proudly watch.

The Kellys had enough for a six-man football team: left to right, Peggy, Lizanne, Kell, Grace, mother, and Jack, Sr. in backfield.

Both outstanding athletes, Lizanne, left, and Peggy ignored acting careers for married life and motherhood.

Cover girl Grace Kelly.

Margaret Kelly breaks ground for new wing at Woman's Medical College of Philadelphia. Mrs. Kelly has been one of the college's leading lights for more than twenty-five years.

Jack, Sr., selected Philadelphia's best-dressed man on several occasions, escorts Sophie Tucker out of theatre during charity affair in which the famous singer performed.

Here's a picture of That Kelly Family taken in the late 1940's. Sitting, left, Grace, mother, Jack, Sr., and Peggy. Standing, left, Kell, Lizanne, and George Davis.

Grace and Marlon Brando congratulate each other after winning Oscars in 1955.

More congratulations, this time from the John B. Kellys who beamed with pride as Grace and Prince Rainier, 3rd, of Monaco announced their engagement in Philadelphia, January 5, 1956.

Princess Grace and father arrived at St. Nicholas, Monaco, amidst brilliant pageantry and ceremony, reminding viewers of a scene out of a fairy tale.

And they lived happily ever after . . .

Homecoming

Kell's homecoming was a gesture of love and appreciation on the part of everyone concerned, a spontaneous reaching out to a young hero who had vindicated a wrong of another era, to thank him for having done so.

It was a day of sparkling sunshine and cheers, bunting and band music, a great and warm-hearted crowd, and fine speeches. Only "The Virginia Judge" could have done the scene justice as Kell and Jack docked in New York upon their return from England. The Kelly women, Mrs. Kelly, Grace and Lizanne, had gone on to Switzerland to recuperate from the Henley excitement, so it was strictly a stag reception.

Chroniclers of Irish lore have tried for ages to capture in print the special quality, the pure body and flavor, of the mother country, but they have not always succeeded. The human eye and ear are wonderful mechanisms, but not so wonderful that they can capture the complex emotions that make up an Irish celebration. The reporter's pencil may catch a phrase and corner it, but something escapes in the translation from eye and ear to notebook and typewriter.

More than 200 prominent gentlemen had roared up from Philadelphia to be at dockside and lift their newest Olympian figure aloft. There was Mayor Bernard Samuel, along with his New York counterpart, William O'Dwyer, and, of course, Grover Whalen, Bigtown's official greeter who has met 'em all. But where were the Governors, Senators and Representatives of Pennsylvania and New York, and where were the British and Irish Ambassadors? Where, in fact, was the President of the United States? They should have been there. Just about everybody else was.

The welcoming committee, all 200 of 'em, were quick to grasp Kell's hand and pump it enthusiastically. Unlike his father, who loved gay scenes and festival, Kell flushed with embarrassment at this exuberant demonstration of hero worship. He honestly felt that his triumphs, no matter how significant, were not deserving of such noisy hysteria.

The events that followed made Kell's head dizzy. Philadelphia political notables largely comprised the reception entourage, and they were there to give New York a lift at its own game of making heroes feel like kings for a day.

All but Mayor Samuel's negligibly bi-partisan party of twenty-seven were daubed in Kelly-green hats.

Two Pullman cars worth of Democrats and Republicans and one special day coach of East Falls Golf Association members were also at dockside. From Pennsylvania Station they had traveled to Pier 90, at the foot of West 50th, Manhattan, in freshly washed and waxed vehicles from Mayor Bill O'Dwyer's motor pool. They formed a boarding party, and, crashing headlong like ten-ton trucks speeding out of a blind alley, the 83,573-ton Queen Elizabeth was surrounded, pinned down and defeated before the Cunard Line officials and emergency crew in charge of the Royal ship's health and security could begin to defend themselves.

Republicans and Democrats and up-Schuylkill Kellyites, some of whom were leftovers from Jack's political days, swarmed over the decks like locusts. One eye was on Kell and Jack, one eye on the cameras, and all eyes on the political ball. All of the ship's ashtrays, bric-a-brac, biscuits, lifeboats and other choice game for souvenir collectors had been lashed down.

Kell and Jack, ably dragooned by photographers who had snapped Lindbergh, Wrong Way Corrigan, Ruth Elder, Queen Marie, Eisenhower, Nimitz and numerous other grand arrivals through similar ordeals, posed and postured, spoke up and piped down with precision.

The love feasting at the microphone would have fed all Britain if love were nourishing. Only twenty-seven shipboarding permits had been issued, just enough for Mayor Samuel's committee. At least 200 of the visitors made the sundeck aft. Mayor Samuel got separated from his alfalfa fedora.

A New York photographer asked for the Kelly's home address. They gave him the street number on Henry avenue.

"What town?" he barked brusquely.

As the tempo increased, a shore-borne Cunard executive moaned, "Who let 'em all on?"

"That is a question I wish you hadn't asked," lamented his superior, "and one I don't care to have answered."

Well, like all hurricanes that sweep up the Atlantic Coast, the game of fraternal "footsie" eventually blew itself out. Mayor Samuel's contingent caught on too late. They were at a photographic disadvantage without the green caps of the Kelly crowd.

It was all ashore that was going ashore and back into the motor caravan for the ride to New York's City Hall, where Bill O'Dwyer was waiting to extend his blessing—but not a wheel budged until they found the visiting Mayor's hat! Another couple minutes' delay was taken while Kell saw to it that his Pocock shell was safely disembarked and on its way to Detroit, where he had an important national championship race coming up.

On the way to City Hall the curbs were lined four-deep with the curious.

"Must be the United Nations going home," commented one viewer.

At City Hall Plaza, the band drenched the sidewalks of New York with Irish melody. An octet of badges from the New York Police Department filled the air with harmony. Grover Whalen—single-breasted serge, blue shirt, dark tie, fresh shave—introduced the visiting Mayor. Mayor Samuel spoke well of Philadelphia and the Kellys. Then Mayor O'Dwyer stood up and spoke well of the Kellys and the Irish.

Jack Kelly admitted that had he been given a chance to pull for the big prize in the old days he would have had an unfair advantage because he had "worked with my hands." He confessed he had no claim to being a *gentleman* at the time. He owned up to a tear or two when Kell had it in the bag in the last quarter of the Henley racing course. He finished with a paternal purr over a son "with whom I am well pleased."

But it was Kell himself who won the oratorical blue ribbon, except he forgot the first name of the Norwegian oarsman he beat in the finals. As a matter of fact, from start to finish over Manhattan's famed "Welcome Home" avenue, Kell stroked himself with precision, catching nary a crab.

O'Dwyer lost the East Falls Irish vote en bloc when he

forgot to call on Terence Beatty, president of the East Falls Golf Association!

The police octet, in a concluding number, let go with the National Anthem, and for a recessional inquired melodiously, "Has Anybody Here Seen Kelly?" By that time, who hadn't. A New York detective whispered, "Where can I swipe one of them green hats?"

It was a grand day for the Irish—and such Philadelphia Democrats and Republicans as may still be groping about in the hold of the Queen Elizabeth, trying to find the escape hatch.

How Walter Kelly would have loved to have been there.

From New York the Kelly entourage returned to Philadelphia, where a homecoming celebration that ended all homecomings was waiting. Thousands lined the streets as the automobile caravan carrying Kell wound and crept its way along the pathway. Flags and banners and colorful bunting flew from every house and store, and homes were even adorned with long ribbons of little pennants with the name "Kell" on them.

A huge banquet, sponsored by the City of Philadelphia, had been planned, but it had to be postponed until Kell competed in the National Championships at Detroit. The luck of the Irish ran out on the world's champion at Detroit. To the utter astonishment of all the sports world, Kell, making his first start since winning the Diamond Sculls, swamped in choppy waters and a brawny Canadian, Theo Dubois, won. Kell had no alibis. Neither did his dad.

"I was just careless," admitted Kell later.

"Son," Jack said, "if you haven't learned your lesson from this experience, you're beyond teaching. A champion must stay in his boat. If you won them all, you wouldn't know the real joy of winning after coming back from defeat. You'll get another crack at Dubois next week."

Kell entered the Canadian Henley Regatta, at Port Dalhousie, the following week. He beat Dubois by four lengths, gaining back a good chunk of the prestige he had lost at Detroit.

Now, at last, it was the City of Philadelphia's turn to officially roll out the red carpet for Kell. On the night of Wednesday, July 30, at the Bellevue Stratford, Mayor Bernard Samuel honored the young hero with a huge testimonial dinner. If it takes all sorts of people to make up the world, then all the world must be here already. Because the arts, the sciences, the drama, commerce, politics, the bench, the clergy, the bar—all these were on hand. A calling over of the names of those in attendance would have sounded like the first hundred pages of Greater Philadelphia's Who's Ballyhoo.

The Kellys were there intact—Jack and Kell, handsome and strong; and Mrs. Kelly, Peggy, Grace and Lizanne, fresh as budding shamrocks. Faith, and they were 'aving a 'igh ol' time.

A tape-recording of the evening's speech-making was made, and, for the sake of posterity, the script went something like this:

TOASTMASTER FRANK TRUSCOTT: "Immediately after the thrilling news was flashed from England that John B. Kelly, Jr., had won the Diamond Sculls, Mayor Samuel and a number of the champion's friends were of one mind—that something should be done by the City of Philadelphia in recognition of his great exploit. The Mayor immediately wired congratulations to the champion and organized a committee, honoring me with its chairmanship, and directed us with full speed ahead to plan a reception for the champion when he arrived back in this country, to be followed by a dinner.

"I have participated in one way or another in receptions to dignitaries who have made marked achievements in many parts of the world and who have visited our city. But I never knew of one that met with a more spontaneous response than the announcement that young John B. Kelly, Jr., would be the city's guest of honor tonight. The Mayor's office was swamped with letters, telegrams and telephone calls.

"Young Jack is probably the most popular champion that this city, or this state, or even this nation, has ever known (applause). And I make no apologies to his famous father, the immortal Jack Kelly, when I make that statement (applause).

"Here assembled tonight are many who have known this young champion from infancy. They watched him down through the years. They have kept in touch with his rowing progress, under the able coaching of his dad. I now have the pleasure of introducing to you a friend of the family of long standing, who is himself one of the outstanding men in this sport. He was the world's champion in 1928, and again in 1930. He has been the rowing coach at LaSalle High School, and coach of the Vesper Club, from which the young champion hails. Here he is—Charles J. McIlvaine."

CHARLIE McILVAINE: "Our community of East Falls is in the habit of building world's champions. Jack Kelly, Sr., and Paul Costello started it all in 1920, when they won the Olympic Championship at Antwerp, Belgium. Since that time, Jack has been an inspiration, not only to the rowing men of East Falls, but also to golfers, swimmers, baseball players and others. His sincerity, his method of training, his diligent work, has brought many champions to our town. Young Kelly is probably the greatest we've ever had. I say this with all due respects to the senior Jack because I have rowed with him, I have seen him row many times against the best in the world. I have also followed young Kell, and to my mind he is the greatest oarsman that ever sat in a boat (applause)."

TOASTMASTER TRUSCOTT: "Thank you, Charlie. In order that this dinner might be paid for, it was necessary that we put on the program the chairman of the City Council's Finance Committee (laughter). And here he is, the Honorable Wallace Egan (applause).

HON. L. WALLACE EGAN: Mr. Toastmaster, guest of honor, mother of the guest of honor, gracious Margaret Kelly—that lady who possesses both the wisdom of Minerva and the charm of Venus—our guest's father, John B. Kelly, Sr., the lovely sisters of our guest, Peggy, Lizanne and Grace.

"I deeply appreciate the privilege of speaking here tonight, because, among other reasons, I happen to have the honor of being president of the Undine Barge Club, a rowing organization which is a member of the Schuylkill Navy, and is now more than ninety-one years old on Boathouse Row. I should likewise be pleased if I might classify myself as an oarsman of another day, but unfortunately there always appears before me the haunting spectacle of a race in which I participated in 1917, where I dragged the members of my crew so far behind our opponents that the spectators on the bank broke forth in a mighty cheer, thinking we were ahead in the next race (laughter).

"Many of you know, some others of you do not, that rowing is a gruelling sport. The period of training begins in bleak winter, first on machines and then on the river, often in rain, in snow, and in bitter cold. There are no cheers in practice. It demands of youth of strength, of courage, of stamina. Many very early, and others quite easily, are discouraged.

"Our guest of honor has far surpassed even the most

exacting type of normal training, because you well know that he started this back when he was only seven years old. With all he has accomplished, and with all the honor he has brought to Philadelphia, it seems to me that one other achievement of his is of equal creditability: he carried on the saga of a rowing family; the toga of his sire was handed to the off-spring, and he acquitted himself well, and wore it with still greater, if unbelievable, glory.

"Through all these years, ladies and gentlemen, he had the inspiration of a loving mother, who gave him maternal inspiration and encouragement. What his father did in aiding him by his tutelage, his skill, and his experience, I find no urge to properly describe. Oh, how proud they must be here tonight, joining with us—with all Philadelphia, with all America, with all the world where rowing is known.

"Kell, I finish by saying to you that we give you credit, and you in turn are a credit to all. We thank you for what you have done."

TOASTMASTER TRUSCOTT: "Thank you, Wally. It takes two to make a bargain, and it takes more than one to make a champion. The gracious mother of the champion we honor tonight has played no small part in bringing him to the pinnacle of his fame. I am now going to call upon that gracious lady, Mrs. John B. Kelly (applause).

MRS. JOHN B. KELLY: "Mr. Toastmaster, Mayor Samuel, Kell, and friends. You certainly must realize that the Kellys are just bursting with pride. And now this wonderful celebration tonight, and to think that it is all for our Kell. Well, words are quite inadequate to describe my emotions tonight. Of course, a celebration of this kind could really only take place in America. Thank goodness we are in America (applause).

"I feel very humble and very happy to witness your enthusiastic appreciation of Kell's victory, to realize that you appreciate the many hours of training, the many hours of sweating and grunting and calloused hands, because that's what it takes to win at Henley. As I said, a celebration like this couldn't possibly occur in Europe, and I think newspapers represent the spirit of a country very vividly. When we were in England, the newspapers—you can't even call them newspapers. London had several news sheets, that's all they were, a sheet folded with news. It was drab, uncolorful, undramatic, and our papers here in America are full, they are colorful, they are dramatic, they are interesting. Of course, they have been awfully good to the Kellys over a period of years. They have given the Kellys a great deal of space. It recalls to mind a time when our oldest daughter, Peggy, was at camp years ago. The youngsters evidently had quite a political discussion. The one little girl evidently got cross, and finally remarked, 'It's a pity your dad can't keep his puss off the front page (laughter).' I wonder what that young lady thinks today after the spread Kell has gotten these last few years! (applause)

"Of course, our papers, shall I say, exaggerate a bit, kind of twist the truth slightly? An instance occurs to me that happened years ago during the war when Victory Gardens were quite the rage, and it was Jack's inspiration that got the Park Commission to allow the people to use gardens there. He came home and said, 'We have to have the best Victory Garden in the neighborhood.' By that time I had already planned the garden, dug up the extra lawn space, had raised the seeds in the little greenhouse, and was ready to transplant them. So one Sunday afternoon—of course, Kell was rowing, Jack was playing golf, and the girls were drifting around somewhere—I decided to cultivate the garden, get a little exercise. I had given up golf for gardening, and worked pretty hard for several hours on this particular day. I enjoyed it, of course, but I came in all hot, ready to take a bath and get dressed. I was under the shower. A few minutes later one of the girls came up and said, 'Mother, dad's home and the photographer is downstairs and wants to take pictures.' I said, 'No photographer is going to take my picture while I'm under the shower.' I didn't want to take the time then to go downstairs. The next day, across the page of the newspapers, was a picture with poppa and the Kelly girls in the garden with hoes and rakes (laughter)!

"After the girls and I arrived from Switzerland last week we were very anxious to see all of Kell's clippings. So we went through them, and there was one there that particularly struck me. It was young Mr. Kelly sprawled out in his chair by his desk with his bare feet on the chair, and the caption read, 'Kelly relaxing after looking over his mother's roses and mowing the lawn (laughter).'

"I can assure you that the first ten years of Kell's life were practically under my influence, and that influence probably has lasted a few more years than that. When Kell was thirteen, he actually did mow the lawn at Ocean City (laughter). But these last ten years I can tell you he has been under his father's influence and jurisdiction (laughter). And I don't think there has been any lawn mowed (laughter).

"But, of course, Kell is a chip off the old block. He follows his father's footsteps, and if what the papers say is true, Kell, you will be a millionaire, and multi-millionaire by some of the papers, and you will be able to afford to have your lawn cut (laughter).

"Now I would publicly like to congratulate my husband—not because he gave his time and effort to train and coach Kell, but because he and many other men, like Charlie McIlvaine, have given of themselves and their time to sponsor schoolboy rowing. They have made it possible for young men to keep their bodies strong and healthy, and when these men give of themselves, they deserve a lot of credit, because schoolboy racing is at its peak in the Schuylkill Navy. So my hat is off to you men, and I hope you continue to give these young men your time and your ability.

"Now, Kell, I have a little gift for you tonight. It is a medal. It is not a gold medal but a bronze one. But it signifies something that I think is very wonderful. It has been picked up from a collection of outstanding medals and plaques and art work. It was beautifully designed. It commemorates an outstanding artist, outstanding sculptor and educator—none other than R. Tate McKenzie. When I taught physical education at the University of Pennsylvania, he was head of the Department at that time.

"This medal pictures three athletes going over a hurdle, and it is called, 'The Joy of Effort.' Many of us have certainly enjoyed effort, and we're happy tonight, Kell, to be here and join the effort you put forth to win the Henley Regatta. I hope you will prize this medal, and I hope that the future hurdles in your life will be cleared as gracefully and successfully as you cleared the Henley hurdle (applause as Mrs. Kelly presents the medal to Kell)."

TOASTMASTER TRUSCOTT: "Now we know one of the ingredients in the recipe for making a champion. Having heard from the distaff side, I should like to introduce to you —rather, present to you, because he needs no introduction— the father of the guest of honor, our beloved John B. Kelly (applause)."

JOHN B. KELLY: "Mr. Toastmaster, Mayor Samuel, friends. First, I want to thank Mayor Samuel, his committee, and all of you for your presence here tonight. Most of you fathers can probably appreciate my feelings at this moment. You kids who are here will not realize it until later.

"But to have an affair of this kind, as Margaret said, could only happen in America, because this banquet is being put on by my former political opponents (laughter).

"I can turn back my memory tonight twenty-seven years, at which time Mayor Moore put on the same kind of celebration for me. I see Charlie Grakelow out there. I think he was chairman of the committee and banquet we had that evening. The city gave me a medal, too, which has always been my favorite medal, and I like Philadelphia because of that spirit.

"And now, Kell, I want to say to you that with all this glory and credit which you are receiving and have earned goes a tremendous amount of responsibility. The youth of the country is watching, and with that responsibility you have to carry on just as you have. Remember that you must pay for all this glory and recognition, for you are an example now and you have to give of yourself the rest of your life. Though you are up at the top, remember that you will get none the best of it. In Detroit, for example, you didn't get any of the best of that, because I talked to the referee after the race and he said, 'Nobody could have stayed in that boat. Two waves happened to hit him at the same time and he was swamped under and went down.' He asked me, 'What did you think of it, Mr. Kelly?' I said, 'A champion has to stay in his boat and win.' Well, the next week Kell had a chance, and it is very lucky he was racing against the same field in Canada as he met in Detroit so he could rub out that defeat, because, otherwise, I think there might have been a damper on tonight's party (laughter).

"The reason I am giving you this little lecture now, Kell—which I probably will do in your own room some night anyway—is that some fellow sent you a telegram which I thought was very clever. It said, 'All sunshine or all shadow does not make a good picture.' All sunshine does not make a good picture, but a little shadow here and there helps. And so when you hit the bottom, it just makes you know you are human and you have to tighten your belt, and when the clouds are at the lowest, you are going through the crucible of life. That's what sport teaches us, that all glory is not the best thing. You wouldn't know how to lose if you won everything. I want you to know how to lose and how to win, so that you can appreciate how the other fellow feels. That's the reason why next week you will be pushing a wheelbarrow full of bricks (laughter). I want you to know life in all its phases, and then you will be worthy of this tribute that you are getting tonight.

"But I do want you to know that you have given me great happiness. You were able to do what I wasn't able to do. Of course, these fellows say that you are much better than I was, but you must realize that perhaps I didn't have as good as coach as you have (laughter). You see, I am a very modest sort of fellow (laughter).

"There has been a great deal said about me being out for revenge. I wasn't out for any revenge. The fact that they had odd rules at that time can't be helped. It just happened I didn't know the rule at that time, and they followed it, and it was all right. I was denied the privilege that I wanted to have, but I wasn't out for revenge. But I did want to see if we couldn't have John B. Kelly on the remaining major rowing trophy in the world (applause).

"I kind of like these banquets, and I hope we have another one next year."

TOASTMASTER TRUSCOTT: "After listening to the father and the mother of the champion, for the life of me I don't see how he can help but be a champion."

Followed by more speeches, another presentation or two, it was finally Kell's turn to speak. And, to the tune of "The Name of Kelly Will Rule for Many a Day," sung by Kelly Streeters, he got to his feet, accompanied by thundering applause.

KELL: "Thank you very much. The Mayor says he hopes

I will remember this night. I don't see how I can ever forget it. No kidding, everybody in this town has been so swell to me I just don't know what to say. I really want to tell you this is the greatest day in my life, even greater than the day I won the Diamond Sculls.

"Most of you fellows here are fathers, and I would like to tell you how my dad got me interested in rowing, and maybe some of you can get your sons interested in a sport in which you would like them to excell.

"I know when I first started out, when I was real young, I thought this rowing was pretty good stuff. I started out as coxswain and used to row in doubles with my dad. I really wasn't nuts about it, but I was interested (laughter). Anyway, after a couple of years of that I became a coxswain and steered a couple of races, and I really got a couple of thrills out of steering two winning crews.

"Then came the years when I got too heavy to be a coxswain and too young and too light to be an oarsman. That was the period when I sort of lost interest in rowing. I was rather fat at the time. I had scarlet fever when I was eleven and I had to sit around and do nothing for a year, and I got a little heavy. They used to call me 'Fat Stuff.'

"When I was thirteen, fourteen, fifteen, around that age, dad wouldn't let me row in races. In fact, there wasn't much competition around because of the war. Dad used to tell me, 'Get out on that river and row that boat.' I really didn't have a great love for it, and I couldn't see it. That's where Ocean City came in. I used to go down every summer. When I was fifteen, I became a life guard down there and started rowing those lifeboats. I think that's the one thing that made me what I am today.

"Tommy Williams, our Captain at Ocean City, had a lot of trouble with me. During the war, they had certain restrictions. They didn't like fellows rowing out very far because of the submarine danger. But one afternoon a pal of mine and I went for a row. It's a wonder I didn't get fired. Tommy Williams laid me off for only ten days. I got in a couple of other scrapes, too, like breaking a couple of boats, but old Tommy didn't fire me. I nevertheless learned a lot down there. It gave me a lot of strength. Pulling those heavy boats all the time through the heavy surf was a great thrill to me.

"When I was sixteen, in 1943, I rowed in my first important race. I rowed with a boy named Sims Drain, a local boy from Ocean City. I really didn't think we had much chance to win. I thought we would be second because there were two monsters against us. But we managed to come through, mainly, I think, because we were in good condition. We trained every night. I never trained so hard in my life, and I think that gave me the code I have lived by since: lots of sleep, good food, and hard work. Anyway, I managed to win that race and was thrilled, and from then on rowing was my sport.

"One thing I want to tell you fathers here who have sons. Don't press them into a sport. Set it up so he can do it, and if he wants to do it he will. I had every opportunity to row, and, as I said, when I was fourteen or fifteen I didn't really have the great desire to do it because there wasn't much competition right then. But what I say to you is, give your sons the opportunity to do it and let them choose the sports they want. I know I am just lucky that I like rowing, and dad is lucky I like rowing, because I might have liked chess, or ping pong, or something like that (laughter).

"I guess you might have read about my little misfortune in Detroit, and I think Mayor Samuel was a little worried about it because he was sort of in charge of this thing to-night. Had I not come through in Canada it would have been pretty bad (laughter). However, I managed to get the fellows up there.

"A lot of stories were printed about what happened out in Detroit, and I will tell you all I can about it, but it happened so fast I really don't recall exactly the details myself.

"It was rather a rough day, as it is in Detroit almost every day. We were rowing up to the starting line, and it seemed that our race attracted extra attention. There were a lot of speed boats wanting to follow our race. So as we all lined up, all these speed boats came up the river, got around behind us, and the race started off. I think they might have waited a few minutes until the wash calmed down a little, because it was really like an ocean out there. Joe McIntyre, who had won the qualifying heat for the championship the day before—you see, each year in the American Championship you are allowed one more man to enter it, and that's to keep a lot of so-called bums off the course. I won that last year and Joe won it this year. He was in the first lane and I was in the second lane. Joe Angyal from New York was in lane three, and this Dubois from Canada was in lane four. We all lined up, and it was rough. We started off. Joe McIntyre and I got a good start, and after ten strokes we were out in front. Then Joe started to get all fouled up with washes. His boat looked like a cork. It was terrific. He started to fall behind and I managed to splash my way slightly ahead. At the end of the first quarter mile I was two lengths in front, Angyal was in second place, and Dubois next. All of a sudden I looked up to see the referee's boat, and he was waving his hands like mad trying to direct traffic. I got a little mental lapse, I guess, but only for a few moments. On my recovery, as I shot my hands away on this one stroke, my oar got fouled up and I went over before I knew it. Well, I let out some language I had never used before (laughter). But now that I think of it, it was pretty bad, but at the time I didn't even think. I was mad at myself.

"We decided that the next week we were going to get those fellows. So we went up to Canada, but we took a smaller squad this time. We only took those that we thought had a very good chance of winning. When we got up there I really took probably the worst ear-lacing of my life. Every kid started yelling 'Hey, Kelly, are you going to turn over today?' It was quite embarrassing.

"Since I have been home I have seen a few cartoons where you see the end of a boat sticking up and a little bird sitting on it and asking, 'Has anybody here seen Kelly?' I was lucky I only had to wait a week to even the score with Dubois.

"But I guess you really want to hear more about the race in England, because that's really what I'm getting this big blast about tonight (laughter).

"Well, we got over there about four days before the Regatta started. The first day out I was very shakey in my boat. I hadn't rowed the boat for two weeks. We packed it before we even sailed, so I was unable to row in it for about two weeks. It was just like learning to row all over again.

"I remember some of the English writers in their stories said, 'The American Kelly arrived today, but his form does not look nearly so good as last year.' I admit it didn't that first day, because I was rowing on a rowing machine going over on the boat, which is nothing like actual rowing in a shell, but it just keeps you in some kind of physical condition, although it doesn't help your form at all. So when we got to England, I rowed twice a day for a few days, and finally I felt like my old self. In fact, I got better after each preliminary heat. A lot of fellows would think you would get weaker after rowing four straight days, but I was improving each day and by that last day I really was what I consider in my top condition.

"Henley, which is thirty miles up the river from London, is a beautiful little town of about 5000 people, but around the Henley Regatta time, as dad told you, there were more than 40,000 there. I don't know how they get there, but they do. Think of it, thirty miles up the river from London, and 40,000 people got there! It is a great regatta, very well run, and it is really the most scenic place I have ever seen in my life, like the Kentucky Derby in this country. People turn out in their best clothes, and the girls in their fineries look like an Easter parade. All the races start right on the button.

"We had sixty-some races the first day. Every five minutes you see that rocket go up, and you could set your watch by it. They always shoot the rocket at the start to let the folks down at the finish line know that the race has started. Dad already has told you how the announcer goes on from one-quarter mile to the next describing the race. Well, as you might have seen in Life Magazine, you can get some idea of the race course. It is absolutely straight for a mile and five-sixteenths. You row up the river and against the wind, so your times are not usually good. The only time you can break the record is when the wind is with you and the current is slack. But conditions weren't like that. We had a lot of water coming down.

"I won my preliminary heats rather easily, and on the fourth day I found myself in the final against Carl Fronsdal of Norway. That was a big day. I kept telling myself as I went to the line, 'Kelly, this is your day. You've got to get it. Everybody back in America is looking for this one, and especially dad.' I started saying my Novenas and everything else. I went on up there to start.

"Everything went as I had planned it. I got off well, and

I was in the best condition of my life. I went down there in great style, and I was really tickled pink as I started going down the last quarter and heard the Englishman yell, 'Well sculled, Kelly.' They really are great sports. No matter who wins, if you do it fair and square, they're all for you.

"After flashing across the finish line, I couldn't wait to get over and shake my dad's hand because I was really happy for his sake that I was able to win this one. As long as I can remember he has told me, 'The Diamond is the one I want, Kell.' I'm certainly proud I got it for him. For America . . . for Philadelphia . . . and, especially, for East Falls."

The next day Jack showed that he meant what he had told the audience about Kell pushing a wheelbarrow. A student of Kingsley, it was Jack's conviction that by starting his son out as a plain apprentice bricklayer would, by force, breed in the boy temperance and self-control, diligence and strength of will, cheerfulness and contentment, and a hundred other virtues that the idle never know.

This theory possibly had been influenced by what Jack once read about two men sharing a seat on a train. One of them was easily eighty years old, but still carbonated with energy and a healthy philosophy. His eyes twinkled.

The other occupant, a man of about forty-five, asked, "What is your secret of eternal youth?"

The old gentleman smiled, and replied, "I'm living on the interest of a well-invested boyhood."

Shortly after the victory dinner, Kell bumped into Ed Pollock on the boardwalk at Ocean City. The Philadelphia sports writer said, "I guess you'll be spending the rest of the summer here at the shore, eh, Kell?"

"Oh, no," Kell said, "I'm down just for the week end. I have to wheel bricks for dad during the week."

Pollock collared Jack later and asked, "Is that right, Jack? Is Kell really pushing bricks?"

"Certainly," Jack said, "and he's going to keep doing it the rest of the summer. Rowing is secondary now. His business career is first. He'll learn this business from the ground up. He's had his fun and his college education. I worked and rowed when I was his age. So can he."

After Kell graduated from Penn in 1950, he became an apprentice bricklayer. When a reporter asked him what his occupation was, Kell squared his shoulders proudly and said, "I'm a bricklayer. I'm a bricklayer by trade and it's a family tradition. All I heard in England was how the bricklayer's son was going to make good for his dad. They made quite a thing out of it. What they missed was that a bricklayer himself won the Diamond."

It was truly a big year for Kell in 1947. As a fitting climax, he was awarded the James E. Sullivan trophy, voted by 600 sports writers and athletic officials throughout the United States. It is the highest honor an amateur athlete can receive. In eighteen years this was only the second time an oarsman had won it. Joe Burk, another single sculler, won the Sullivan Award in 1939.

From Sullivan to Burk to Kelly. Let anybody try to intercept that one!

Kell was in Florida for the Palm Beach Regatta, to row singles and was visiting Harry Whitney, stepson of Averill Harriman, the present New York governor, when he learned of winning the Sullivan Award. This was during the Christmas holidays at Hobe Sound, fifteen miles northeast of Palm Beach, and he was sitting at the breakfast table when Mr. Harriman walked in and slapped him on the back.

"Congratulations, son," said Mr. Harriman.

"What for?" asked Kell, puzzled.

"Why, for winning the Sullivan Award, of course," said Mr. Harriman.

Everybody had heard the news on the radio, but Kell!

That evening Kell attended a dance on the deck of a

millionaire's yacht along with oarsmen from the Penn and Yale crews. A pretty girl walked over to him and asked, "Are you on one of the crew teams?"

Because he rowed singles, he decided that he wasn't and wig-wagged his head.

"No, I'm not," he said.

"A fellow with your build ought to be able to make the crew easily," cooed the girl. "Why don't you try out for crew?"

Actually, Kell did row in the Penn varsity eight during his junior and senior years, 1949 and 1950.

Toward the end of the Forties, the name, the figure, and above all, the honest engaging personality of Kell became welded into the national sports scene. Came spring, came Kell. Came Kell, came the rowing season and victory after victory. His string ran on. Week in week out he rowed, sick or well, never missing a race.

Because of the Olympic Games, which he lost, Kell didn't compete at Henley in 1948, but he returned in '49 and won the Diamond Sculls again with a smashing triumph over his opponent. It was the most lop-sided victory in the event's history.

From Henley, Kell toured Europe, competing in exhibitions. The world's champion was much in demand. His dad was too busy to go to Europe with him that summer, but Jack made sure that Kell had a traveling companion. Joe Flanagan, one of Kell's pals from Philadelphia, went along to keep the champion amused and relaxed. Flanagan could do that all right. He was a colorful character, with plenty of the Rover Boy in him.

Before the two young globe trotters pushed off, Jack took Flanagan aside and said, "Joe, I want you to keep an eye on Kell's rowing. I have written down some instructions. Study them and then see that Kell follows them. I feel if you can speak the language he will listen to you. I'm counting on you."

"Don't worry, Mr. Kelly, I will take care of him," assured Flanagan.

When the ship docked in Europe, the boys were met by newspaper reporters. Flanagan took charge immediately. He told them that he was Kell's coach. It even made the papers.

In Paris, they rented a 1937 Ford, toured France, Switzerland and Belgium, where Kell won races in each country, and then flew on to Amsterdam. There they picked up a 1932 Ford and seriously went to work. Kell was rowing in the European Championships.

Kell tuned up on a special man-made canal in Holland. A road had been built alongside the canal so that automobiles could follow the racing shells. The mornings Kell took his practice spins the road was jammed with vehicles and bicycles, out to get a glimpse of the world's champion.

Flanagan sat on the hood of the Ford, wearing Burmuda shorts and a baseball cap, and shouted instructions. One of his girl friends he had picked up along the way drove.

"You're shootin' your butt!" roared Flanagan. "You're dippin' your hands before the catch!"

And so it went, all the way down the course.

After workouts, in the boathouse, European coaches flocked around Flanagan asking advice.

The Swiss mentor wanted to know what Joe thought of Switzerland's chief entry. "A good boy," Flanagan said authoritatively, "but he did appear to be a little late on the catch, and he was sloppy on the finish. Tell him to watch it."

The Swiss coach bowed graciously. "Thank you, sir," he said.

Kell, watching Flanagan's performance, smiled to himself and thought, "Look at that Flanagan, will you? These coaches have been connected with rowing all their lives—and Flanagan has been with it all of eight weeks!"

P.S. With Flanagan rooting him in, Kell breezed through the European Championships. In the finals he defeated Rissa of Uruguay, the man who defeated him by a tenth of a second in the 1948 Olympics, by eight lengths.

Another victory dinner was waiting for Kell when he returned from winning the Diamond Sculls in 1949, but this time the old gang from East Falls was not invited. So Paddy Neilan and other members from the good old Gunboat days arranged with Godfrey Ford, the Kellys' chauffeur of many years, to have him drive Kell home from the banquet by way of the "Corner."

Godfrey followed instructions. Kell got out of the car and was immediately surrounded by Paddy and his coterie in a solemn ritual as impressive as a Mayan sacrificial ceremony and as immutable as the laws of the Medes and the Persians.

Paddy, the spokesman for the "boys," made what was perhaps the shortest speech of his career.

"We thought you'd like this to remember us by," he said.

It was a gold tie clip and lapel pin. Inscribed on the back was: "From the boys on the corner."

Grace Leaves Home

As a little girl, Grace was plain and shy and not very colorful, completely overshadowed by the gigantic and compelling figures of her famous relatives. In contrast with the others, she was never considered very unusual or outstanding.

Once, while news photographers were snapping pictures of Kell, Grace, who had been standing idly by, suddenly found herself beside her brother as the cameras clicked away. One of the photographers looked up and growled, "What's that blond doing in there? Get her away! Who does she think she is anyway!"

Though Peggy and Lizanne were far more athletic competitively, Grace was Kell's No. 1 rooter. But, as Kell pointed out, don't let Grace's fragile, frosty beauty fool you. A few years ago one of Kell's Marine friends showed Grace some jujitsu holds. In April of 1955, while doing a picture layout for a national slick magazine, she walked up to Photographer Howell Conant, laced her arm around his neck, then reached down, got him by the ankles and tossed him on his back. Staring from a sitting position at the smiling, fragile-looking girl, Conant was amazed.

"I think," Grace said later, "I made him mad."

During the filming of "Mogambo," one of Grace's initial screen triumphs, she flabbergasted other members of the cast while on location in Africa. She dived into heavy surf one day, swam several hundred yards out into the ocean, and then rode a wave into the beach. Apparently, most movie actresses don't do that sort of thing.

Perhaps the story of Grace Kelly, actress extraordinary, begins on the stage of the East Falls "little" theatre with the Old Academy Players. She had one of the lead roles in Uncle George Kelly's "The Torch Bearers."

"The Kellys of East Falls have a new member making a bid for the limelight," wrote one Philadelphia critic the following day. "Grace Kelly, John B.'s pretty daughter, made her pro stage debut last night in Uncle George Kelly's comedy hit, 'The Torch Bearers.' For a young lady whose previous experience was slim, Miss Kelly came through this footlight baptism of fire splendidly. Although father and mother beamed at Grace from the front rows and other friends were scattered through the house, it was largely a theatrical crowd this girl faced on her break-in. From where we sat, it appeared as if Grace Kelly should become the theatrical torchbearer for her family."

Following local successes, the urge to graduate to loftier plateaus plagued Grace until she could stand it no longer. There had been talk of going on to college, but the only schooling she wanted was at the American Academy of Dramatic Arts in New York. It came as no surprise to her father when she asked him for permission to leave home.

"New York?" said Jack.

"Yes," explained Grace, "I want to enroll in the American Academy of Dramatic Arts and study hard to become a real good actress."

Jack more or less had been preparing himself for this moment, when he would have to decide whether or not to let his daughter follow in the same path of his famous brothers, Walter and George.

"It's a dangerous profession, both before and after you reach the top," Jack told her. "If you go into this, you must dedicate yourself to it. You can't be half-way about it. There will be sacrifices, lots of them. While others play, you will have to be getting your rest so that you will look nice the next day. And once you reach the top you become public property. There will be no privacy. The public will make great demands on you. Are you ready to pay the price?"

Jack looked level-eyed at Grace, trying to make her understand the seriousness of the decision.

"Yes," she said finally.

Without further preliminaries, Jack said, "Your mother and I had hoped that you would give up the idea of being an actress. Those movie people lead pretty shallow lives. But if this is what you want, then you have our blessings. Go ahead."

Grace's face was illuminated with triumph.

"Oh, daddy," she cried, "I won't disappoint you."

Jack's ancestors certainly must have been kind to the little people back in Ireland, because God sure has been kind to the last two generations of East Falls Kellys.

So Grace moved to Manhattan, taking up residence at the Barbizon Hotel for Women. To assure her independence, she got a job modeling. She started at seven dollars an hour, had jumped to twenty-five dollars per hour. This was an astronomical fee compared to the five dollars an hour her mother used to make as a top model back in 1919.

Grace also did television commercials. About this phase of her career, she was later to crack, "I was terrible. Honestly, anyone watching me give the pitch for Old Golds would have switched to Camels."

Grace eventually worked her way into television and did very well in dramatic productions. Her thinly drawn blond beauty and a certain discipline of manner were heavily in demand. She displayed rare versatility. In one hectic two-week period, she played three roles: a college girl on Tuesday, a rich girl on Sunday, and, eight days later, a country school teacher. Another time she happily found herself on "Lights Out" portraying a provocative music hall singer in short skirt and black mesh stockings.

Despite her rising success on TV, Grace stubbornly made the rounds of summer stock and casting offices. She read for almost everything that has been cast, even the ingenue part in "The Country Girl" on Broadway, the role which was later left out of the movie.

"Sorry," she was told, "you're too intelligent looking. You just aren't the ingenue type."

That was generally the theme. She was too tall, or too leggy, or too something. She read for forty plays and didn't get a one.

Then she read for the daughter's part in Strindberg's grim "The Father." She got the part. Raymond Massey, a rowing friend of father Jack's, was starring in the play. On the night that Grace made her debut, she brought her parents to a party for the cast. Massey greeted them warmly, but he couldn't figure out why they were there. Grace had never told him that she was the daughter of John B. Kelly.

Grace was completely independent. She took after her Uncle George in that respect. George, who lives in retirement in California today, still single and living off the royalties from his plays, never would permit brother Walter or anyone to help him when he was struggling to crash the theatre. He wanted to earn success on merit, not inside pull.

"George and Grace are alike in many ways," thought Jack to himself, as he watched her perform in her Broadway debut. "She has never allowed any of us to help her. She says that she is going to make good on her own."

Once before and once shortly after she left dramatic school, Grace rejected $250-a-week movie contracts. She didn't want to be just another starlet. Finally, she accepted a bit part in "Fourteen Hours." After completion of the picture, she was offered a contract. Again she turned it down, explaining that she did not feel ready yet.

As soon as "Fourteen Hours" was finished, Grace went right out and bought herself a mink stole. ("It was something I'd always wanted, but couldn't afford before.")

"Fourteen Hours" produced Grace's first fan, a high school girl up in Oregon who organized a fan club and kept Grace posted on new members. Grace couldn't understand why anyone as unimportant as she was at that time, could merit a fan club. Now she loves her clubs and is in constant correspondence with them.

Next came the role of Gary Cooper's young wife in "High Noon." Grace's finishing-school accent sat awkwardly amongst the western drawls, and her fresh beauty made little impact. She began to have doubts about her future.

Thinking about it, she told herself, "Everything is so clear working with Gary Cooper. When I look into his face I can see everything he is thinking. But when I look into my own face I see absolutely nothing. I know what I am thinking, but it just doesn't show. I wonder if I am going to be a great star after all. Maybe I am not any good. I had better go back to New York and learn how to make it show."

This time Grace moved into a two room apartment in Manhattan House, masonry by John B. Kelly, Inc. She was still learning more about her profession when 20th Century-Fox called her to test for a role in a film called "Taxi." They dressed her up in an old skirt and a man's shirt and took her to Gregory Ratoff. He threw his arms up and screamed, "She's perfect! What I love about this girl, she's *not* pretty." But the producer of the film did not like her. Another actress got the part.

Director John Ford later saw Grace in the test she had made in "Taxi," however, and he enthused, "This is no mere beauty. This girl can act. I want her for Mogambo."

When M-G-M offered her a seven-year contract, Grace demanded—and got—a year off every two years for a play, and permission to live in New York, instead of hanging around Hollywood, whenever she finished a picture. She was only twenty-two, and all but unknown, but M-G-M agreed to her demands.

Now the parade was on. Grace landed one good part after another, and folks found themselves standing in long lines—to see, of all things, an actress for whom nobody had beaten the tom-toms of publicity and upon whom no one had squandered the customary millions of dollars. Grace dashed from movie to movie with such rapidity that film row wits came up with this one: "I hear Hollywood is making a picture *without* Grace Kelly."

The female who thought she knew what made men breathe heavily was thrown for a fifteen-yard loss by Grace. Although she is refreshingly easy on the eyes, plenty of more-striking looking actresses were drawing unemployment insurance from the State of California. There was only one conceivable explanation of why Grace was stirring up more excitement in the movie set than any other star of recent years:

Grace Kelly is an exceptionally talented young actress.

In 1954, Grace could not interrupt her movie-making to fly home to attend Kell's wedding. Kell was marrying pretty Mary Freeman, the national swimming champion. They had met during the 1952 Olympic Games in Finland. Both were members of the U.S. Olympic Team. Mary was an extraordinarily well-poised young woman, completely charming, and behind her dewy youth (she was only twenty at the time) was something ageless and wise, yet wholly innocent.

During the Olympics Kell was beaten by one and a half lengths in the semi-finals by Josef Tjukalov. The next day, getting another chance in second-try heats, he was denied the only major sculling title he had never won when Teodore Kocerka, the Polish champion whom Kell beat in opening day heats, nosed him out in a photo finish. This eliminated Kell from the Olympics.

"I thought the Pole would crack," Kell said after the race, "but he didn't. Maybe it's just as well. I don't think I would be up to it tomorrow."

Again Kell showed he could take it as well as dish it out.

Out of fairness to Kell, it should be pointed out that he had been away from rowing for a year and a half while serving as an officer in the Navy. He had plenty of time to practice but no one to coach him or to train against. He wasn't at his best in the 1952 Olympics.

Kell and Mary Freeman hit it off immediately. She was as typical an American girl as he had ever laid eyes on. Like Kell, she was a very determined and strong-minded competitor once she set herself to the task. It was fortunate for her neighbors that she never decided to take up the tuba.

Mary is a caramel blonde with a pert pug nose and a brilliant smile. She has been on the cover of Life Magazine. Mary was discovered at the age of fourteen paddling in a pool at Walter Reed Army Hospital, Washington, D.C., where her father was a staff chemist. Mary could barely swim the length of the pool. She was there only because she was new to Washington and hadn't yet made friends.

Jim Campbell, the hospital's aquatic director and amateur coach, watched Mary and said, "Kid, I like the way you move in the water. I'm going to take you under my wing."

For the next seven years, Mary specialized in the backstroke and medley. She established three National A.A.U. records, won the National Senior Indoor 200-yard backstroke and 300-yard medley championships, competed at Helsinki, and accumulated enough cups and medals to fill her room.

These cups and medals cost Mary every pleasure an extremely pretty, healthy young miss lives for. She seldom had night dates. Late hours do not mix with athletics. Dancing, tennis and basketball were forbidden.

"They would harden my long, relaxed swimming muscles," she explained. During her twice-daily practice sessions, totaling four hours, Mary labored to the point of exhaustion under the eye and tongue of her coach, Jimmy Campbell. She endured endless sprints, countless drills, innumerable corrections, but suffered happily, knowing that is the price the champion must pay. She and Kell had a lot in common.

Between them they owned more championship medals than you can shake a stick at. Competing in his third straight Olympic Games in 1956, Kell's complete record included a total of 131 wins (all types of boats) against only 17 defeats. His singles record was 84-7. His best year was 1953, when he won five National championships, four in one afternoon in 99 degree temperature, and finished the season with 26 victories and no losses. He won the Pan American Olympics in 1955. He had won eight National single titles and six Canadian championships, a record.

And so they were married. At the wedding, Jack offered a toast to Mary and Kell:

"I can understand why women cry at weddings," he said, "but I never could until now. I can remember the day Kell was christened and we opened a bottle of champagne to celebrate the occasion. We were all wishing and hoping and wondering what the world had in store for our first son. I wished that he would one day win the Diamond Sculls, a privilege that I had been denied. His mother and the guests all predicted and hoped for certain events in his life.

"History seems to be repeating itself. The first time I saw Margaret was just as she was diving into the Turner's Pool. She was a swimmer. I was an oarsman. Here we are today, gathered to join Mary and Kell in the biggest event of their lives, and, judging from my experience, this swimmer and oarsman combination seems to be alright. And Kell, if you do as well as I did, you will have no complaint.

"So here's to Mary. May you and Kell glide down the river of life doing an occasional racing start and picking up a few added starters along the way." Kell and Mary are now the parents of two daughters—Ann, born in June, 1955, and Sue, who arrived on the same month a year later.

Meanwhile, back on the West Coast, what exactly Hollywood had in store for Grace in 1954 she knew not. Paramount, it soon developed, asked M-G-M to lend them Grace for "The Country Girl." Jennifer Jones had been scheduled to play the title role, but she had become pregnant and couldn't work. M-G-M said no. Grace had read the script, and she wanted the part terribly. Her ability to know what role is *right* for her always has been remarkable. No one in her family knows where she has acquired this sense, but it is there.

"The Country Girl" was final proof that Grace was not merely something enchanting to watch. She was completely convincing as the slatternly, embittered wife of Bing Crosby, who portrayed an aging, alcoholic matinee idol. She slouched around with her glowing hair gone dull, her glasses stuck on top of her head, her underlip sullen, resentment in the very sag of her shoulders and the dangle of her arms. She looked dreadful. Only an *actress* could have made that come through.

Grace gave a terrific performance, but, watching her on the set, George Seaton thought to himself, "I keep feeling she's holding back new and unexplored facets of her talent. That's why she is a great star. There always will be something new about her in every picture."

Grace won an Academy Award nomination with her performance in "The Country Girl." She never seriously felt that she would win the big prize, though. She thought it would go to Judy Garland for her comeback role in "A Star Is Born."

Those were anxious weeks as Grace waited for the zero hour to arrive—the Academy Award ceremony.

She would soon know the verdict.

Oscar Night For Grace

The big hour finally had come and gone. Now every block of the way from the theatre, Grace kept telling herself that it was only a fantastic dream, that any moment now she would wake up. Those incredible words—"And the Best Actress of the Year award goes to," there was a pause, an overwhelming tension built up like electricity in a cloud, gathering itself and waiting to be ignited, and then, Bill Holden, the winner of the year before, said, "Grace Kelly!"

En route to Romanoff's from Hollywood's Pantages Theatre, where the annual Oscar Award was staged, Grace's thoughts remained with the exciting events of an hour ago. She remembered walking slowly up the aisle to the stage of the theatre, taking the shiny bronze statuette that William Holden proffered her, and saying in a soft, broken whisper to a television audience of millions: "I will never forget this moment. W-w-words . . . a-all I can say is—t-t-thank you all." Then, sobbing gently, she walked off into the wings, her face vulnerable as no one had seen it before, her eyes strained and misty. Grace recalled being greeted backstage by a battery of photographers, reporters, and film cognoscente, who conversed, for the most part, with exclamations, hand gestures, and quick displays of teeth.

Marlon Brando was there, too, and one of the photographers had piped up, "Oh, Grace, why don't you kiss Marlon?"

She drew up, and replied archly, showing her breeding even under such emotional circumstances, "Well, I think *he* should kiss me."

The Best Actor of the Year did.

Reaching this night, the biggest night in an actress' career, had been no easy path for Grace. If the public only knew what she had endured to get here—so many hours posing for countless publicity stills, indoor and out; spending hours in a darkened theatre auditioning, and eagerly hearing others read their parts; modeling and taking bit parts until The Break came along. Those long hours of waiting outside the casting office, hoping terribly that she got the part—any part—wanting it so much, and frightened to death that she wouldn't get it. Strange how this world, the world of the theatre, grabbed and held you and wouldn't let go. Indeed there was only one life for an actress—the life of the theatre. It was like a contagious fever, but Grace wouldn't have it any other way. She had made the grade, her name was in lights—the Actress of the Year—and there was no reward to compare.

In contrast to other stars, however, Grace had become a headliner practically overnight. How did she explain her meteoric rise? She thought, "I just don't know. I've just had fantastic luck, I guess. That and good agents and many friends in the industry." Only that afternoon she had had dinner with her mother, who had come out to be with her for the Academy Award ceremony, over at Paramount Studios, and people kept coming to the table wishing her luck.

Bing Crosby, for example, came over and said, "Good luck, Gracie. We're keeping our fingers crossed for you."

And William Perlberg, co-producer of "The Country Girl," had added, "Everybody's rooting for you."

"That's very sweet and thoughtful of them," her mother told her. "No one made them come over here and say those nice things. They did it because they wanted to."

Rich girl makes good! That's a plot Hollywood script writers would regard as too ridiculous to bear comment. Not even in the movies do such things happen. It's the sort of folderol that gives fiction a bad name. But Grace was just that: a rich girl who had struck it rich, the daughter of John B. Kelly, millionaire contractor of Philadelphia. She wondered what her father was thinking.

Back in East Falls, Pennsylvania, Jack Kelly permitted a smile to settle on his countenance, casting his mind back over the years and thinking of a thousand things. Some friends had come over to watch the Oscar show on television, and afterward Jack said, shaking his head, "I can't believe it. I simply can't believe Grace won. Of the four children, she's the last one I'd expected to support me in my old age." A psychiatrist, he thought, would find plenty of significance in the facts of Grace's childhood—the inner struggle that his daughter's ambitious spirit had waged against her self-doubt, her supersensitiveness and—most formidable of all—her near mediocrity of sports talent in a family of champions.

Life for the Kellys certainly had been varied enough, Jack thought. Drawing a deep breath, he let his gaze drift around the large, comfortable living room of the red-brick, fifteen-room home he had personally built for his family thirty years ago. His eyes stopped, held by a portrait of Grace, smiling demurely from out of a gold-rimmed frame over on the piano, and a feeling of enormous pride swelled up inside him. She had climbed to the top on her own, without any help from home. From the time she was six, and performing minor parts in home theatricals organized by Peggy, the oldest daughter, Grace wanted only to be on the stage. Though she enjoyed tennis, swimming and horseback riding, athletically she was never as active as her brother, Kell, and sisters, Peggy and Lizanne. Yet she was Kell's most enthusiastic rooter.

Jack thought of the afternoon, back in 1950, when Mervin Wood, Australia's Olympic champion of 1948, and the 1950 Diamond Sculls winner, Tony Rowe, raced Kell on the Schuylkill River in The Philadelphia Gold Cup. Jack had won this coveted event himself in 1920, the first year it was held, and Kell had dreamed of duplicating his father's performance. But, handicapped by a severe cold, he finished second. Sick, dejected, his body aching, Kell showered in silence, and then returned home. Grace was waiting for him. The instant he opened the door she ran up to him, flung her arms around his neck, and started to cry. Kell looked helpless. Pleading to his mother, he said, "Try to get her to stop, mom. After seeing her cry like this I feel worse for her than I do for myself."

Thinking about the incident, Jack smiled.

And what about the time when she was only eleven years old and had landed a role in a show presented by the Old Academy Players of Philadelphia. In the second act, her stage mother muffed her lines. With characteristic coolness, Grace dropped her handbag, turned her back on the audience, and gave the older actress her lines, while she, Grace, was picking up her bag.

Jack had been sitting in the front row that evening, and turning to his wife, he beamed, "Margaret, we've got a trouper on our hands."

Back in those kindergarten days in dramaturgy, Grace always went to rehearsals, no matter how sick she was. If the production needed expensive clothes for props, Grace obliged by borrowing her mother's.

Despite her shyness off-stage, she had all the poise, ability and charm in the world once the curtain went up. Everything about her made people think Grace was seventeen when she was only fourteen. She had to fib about her age to get a part in one show. She was twelve, but the role called for a fourteen-year-old. The director had said, "Grace, you know you're really a big girl for your age." She had looked at him shyly and said, "I have to tell you I lied about my age. I am only twelve, but I am ashamed of being so young." There was a sparkle in Jack's eyes as the story came back to him, and he thought, "Grace is one woman who will never be able to fib about her age, not as long as that cement in our driveway sticks together." Imprinted boldly in the cement is the inscription: "Grace is fourteen today, November 12, 1943."

A deeply understanding girl, Grace, once when an older member of the Old Academy Players was trying to get her daughter to wear darned nylons to keep the family budget down, broke in and said, "I wear nylons and they are darned, too." Whereupon she displayed her skillfully stitched stockings. Later, a star, she relaxed between scenes by knitting socks for her leading men—"Gable's feet are so big it took me five months to knit him a pair."

Watching Bill Holden hand Grace her Oscar, Jack smiled to himself, "That Holden not only is a great actor, he's also a pretty amazing prophet."

The year previous, while Mrs. Kelly was visiting Hollywood, Holden had invited her over to his studio dressing room.

"Congratulations, Bill, for winning the Academy Award," Mrs. Kelly had said.

The actor grinned broadly.

"Mrs. Kelly," he said, "I predict that a year from now I'll be back on that stage giving your daughter an Oscar of her own."

Grace had been nominated for the Best Supporting Actress award for her role in "Mogambo," and when she didn't get it the crew from Paramount who had worked with her had a special plaque made for her with the inscription:

"You are still our Oscar Winner, and this will hold you 'till next year."

Jack was shaken from his reminiscence by the doorbell. Rising, he crossed the room. Outside stood a Western Union boy. Jack's complexion glowed with pleasure as he read the telegram, which had been sent to him by a Philadelphia friend, General Baker.

"Congratulations," he read. "The Country Girl has become the girl of the country."

The clock in the hallway struck twelve and Jack walked slowly up the stairs to bed. Indeed, it had been another exciting night in the lives of the Philadelphia Kellys.

Life Rolls On

Lizanne, the youngest of the Kelly children, spent all her summers in Ocean City. It was there she met Donald Le-Vine, a lifeguard and former football star of Bethany College. His family lived in Pittsburgh and spent their summers in Ocean City. Like Mr. and Mrs. Kelly, Kell and Mary Freeman, Peggy and George Davis, Liz and Don also met at the waters edge.

It was love at first sight—after six months of courtship, Don proposed, but Margaret and Jack wanted Liz to finish college; she was attending the University of Pennsylvania, so they asked them to wait until Liz received her degree.

Well, Liz graduated June 1, 1955, and on her birthday, June 25th, she and Don were married at St. Bridget's Church in the Falls of Schuylkill. Kell was one of the ushers, Peggy, maid of honor, and Grace, one of the bridesmaids. The church was filled to capacity. The local police had a problem with the crowds who lined Midvale Avenue.

The night before the wedding Don's mother and father gave a dinner for the wedding party. Everyone was called upon to toast the prospective bride and groom. When Jack was called, he read a poem he had written that day—"With apologies to Rudyard Kipling's 'If.' "

TO DON

If you can keep your head when all the ushers
Are predicting that Lizanne will not show up
If you can trust yourself when these four-flushers
Promise if she don't, they'll share your bitter cup

If you can wait and not grow tired by waiting
And wonder whether Tom still has the ring
And when you think these thoughts, you start debating
Then the butterflies in your stomach all take wing

If you remember Pittsburgh as your dream place
Or wonder if old Bethany is still the same
Dream all you like, my lad, but this you must face
You asked for it, now you have yourself to blame

If you could remember all the words you've spoken
When you promised Liz how constant you would be
She's a gal who doesn't like a promise broken
And she'll remember all you said down by the sea

If you could make a pile of all the money
That you won at Atlantic City and at Garden State
Liz will say, "It isn't very high now is it, Honey?"
And you will say, "Not now, but just you wait"

If you can force your heart and nerve and sinew
To walk the floor at night with babe in arms

This crying kid will try the soul within you
While you look at Liz asleep with all her charms

If you can cope with all Lizanne's relations
Most of whom failed their psychiatric test
Then, too, you may develop some hallucinations
And if it's contagious, you'll be like the rest

If you can take this Kelly Family for a minute
And hear them tell of all the prizes they have won
Then your's is the world and everything that's in it
And I will say, you're a helluva man, my son.

After the wedding, the LeVines drove off in a car, presented to them as a surprise gift, to White Sulphur Springs for their honeymoon.

In May, 1956, a baby girl was born. They were discussing a name for the new arrival when Liz remembered that at the wedding, Grace asked her not to name her first girl Elizabeth Ann, because she liked the name Lizanne so much, she wanted to name her first daughter Elizabeth Ann. So Liz decided that her baby would be called Grace, and she was christened in St. Madeline's Church in Germantown.

The Jack Kellys as men and women have captured the hearts of America. It struck the author, when meeting the family for the first time, that the Kellys, although far better-heeled than most folks, don't need money to enjoy a rich family life. Finding fun in the simplest things, they double it with their delight and pride in one another.

Naturally, the author expected to find the Kellys living in a typical million-dollar mansion complete with huge walls, butlers, and imported chandeliers, something like the castle Princess Grace finds herself in today. What I encountered was a whiff of good, wholesome American home life.

In her quiet way, Margaret Kelly is as remarkable a

woman as her doughty, God-fearing mother-in-law was. Always she has stood loyally, staunchly in the shadow of her famous husband. Bringing up her four children, Peggy, Grace, Kell and Lizanne, in their formative years was her responsibility because civic and sports affairs dominated so much of Jack's time. There were three children in her own Majer family, and they were raised with German discipline, and a strict, devout belief in Christianity. They were taught to be good for good's sake, and to live clean, active and healthy lives. It was with this spirit that Margaret Kelly tried to raise her own youngsters.

All of the Kellys are fine athletes. Peggy was an outstanding swimmer. At fifteen, a couple of the nation's top swimming coaches badgered Jack to let them take Peggy and train her for the Olympics. Grace was a better than fair swimmer, too. Lizanne captained her basketball team at University of Pennsylvania, and stood out on the swimming, field hockey and women's tennis teams.

With Grace's marriage to Prince Rainier III, the four Kelly offspring are all married now.

Peggy's oldest daughter, Meg Davis, ten, apparently has inherited the Kelly athletic talent. For the past two years at Madison Square Garden, this fairy-like bundle of personality has placed high in the junior division of the Eastern Figure Skating Championships. Jack has a favorite anecdote about his granddaughter. When she was two she had the habit of watching the older people play bridge. Feeling left out of things, she would shriek, "Me play, me play, too!"

"Here," she was told, "take these cards and go off in the corner and play by yourself."

So Meg pretended she was playing cards, too. By memorizing the numbers, she got very good at figures. Her Nun at school, a few years later, complimented her one day.

"You are very good at numbers, Meg Davis," the Nun said. "Where did you learn?"

"Oh," said Meg, "I've been playing poker since I was two."

East Falls natives may be excused if they have the notion that Margaret Kelly has had something to do with the invention of the practice of medicine. For twenty-six years now, she has been the devoted, determined leading light of the Woman's Medical College, located within walking distance of the Kelly home. She has learned what a powerful influence a worthwhile project such as Woman's Medical College can exert toward drawing a family together.

Among the fund-raising projects Mrs. Kelly used to sponsor was the annual June Carnival. Here Peggy, Grace, Lizanne and Kell got a chance to participate. As soon as the Kelly flowers bloomed in the Spring, they cut the blossoms from bush and stem, put them in containers of water, and placed them on a little table at the end of their driveway. They made a sign—"Buy Flowers For The Woman's Medical College"—and were open for business. The clearest picture that neighbors have of Grace as a little girl is that of a cute tyke standing in front of the Kelly home selling flowers.

Another project that the Kelly youngsters organized for the benefit of the WMC was a circus on the tennis court in back of their home. The entire neighborhood collaborated, including Mrs. Kelly's brother, who was the Ringmaster. Grace, in her tiny ballet dress, was the bareback rider. Lizanne was the groom for the Tom Thumb bride and groom number, and one of her cousins was the bride. Kell was the strong man, and lifted weights.

At Christmas, the Kellys trimmed the WMC tree. They went on cutting expeditions to woods nearby and "borrowed" greens.

One afternoon, Peggy, then in high school, brought a lot of boys home with her from school. They filed into the basement for cokes and to dance to the record-player. A little later Mrs. Kelly came down, wearing her ski suit and armed with a pair of shears.

"Come on children," she commanded, "get on your coats and hats. We're going to cut greens."

Peggy was scandalized.

"Mother!" she cried, "you *wouldn't* dare ask these boys to cut greens!"

"Sorry, Peggy," said Mrs. Kelly, "but I can't stand to see all this energy go to waste. Come on, boys."

In the Spring of 1955, a week after Grace won the Academy Award, we were having dinner at the Kelly home, and Mrs. Kelly turned to Grace and said she wanted her to serve on the WMC's national fund-raising committee. Mrs. Kelly is vice-president of the Board.

"I will be happy to, Mother," said Grace. "What exactly do you want me to do?"

"I haven't decided yet," her mother said, but it was apparent that the wheels in her head were whirring busily.

Peggy, the wit of the family, had been studying her mother, and she suddenly piped up: "Fund-raising is fund-raising, Mother, but charging folks a buck apiece to come in and look at Grace's Oscar is going too far."

To illustrate how deeply Margaret Kelly's unflagging devotion to Woman's Medical College goes, when a new wing had to be built at the hospital, Kelly For Brickwork, Inc., did it—totally innocent of dividends. Jack says that his wife will not allow him to figure on one penny above costs. The college, she argues, needs the money more than he does.

In June of 1955 Margaret Kelly was awarded an honorary degree (Doctor of Law) from the college. When Jack first heard about it, he grinned, "It was about time they were giving her a Doctor of Law. She has been laying down the law to the Kellys for an awful long time."

There are countless stories about Jack Kelly, amounting

almost to legend, about his never-failing readiness to sacrifice himself in a cause he believes in. But all of the laudatory stories add up to essentially this: If a man lives what he believes, he can and does influence everything around him. Because Jack Kelly has lived what he so sincerely believes, the whole community around him . . . his town, his country, all the world . . . has richly benefited.

Jack keeps a framed poem hanging in his study at home as a constant and vivid reminder of his beliefs and everything he stands for. Once we understand what the words mean to Jack, we get a candid glimpse at the unflinching pattern of his own life. The name of the poem is "Dreams," written by Edgar Guest:

"The things that are were the dreams of old
The work of a few brave men and bold
There's little we own and enjoy today
Not a bulb of light or a level way
But stands as proof of the faithful few
Who dared to dream of what men might do.

"Never by many are marvels wrought
By one or two are the dreams first caught
The throng will follow the easy way
Content to live with its yesterday
And the dreamer shaping a better plan
Must bear the jeers of his fellow man.

"The dreamer must toil when the odds are great
Must stand to failure and work and wait
He must keep his faith though he stand alone
Until the truth of his dream is known
For the crowd will follow its well fixed groove
It's hard to change and it's hard to move

"Dreamers have charted the open seas
And broken the vaults of the centuries

Dreamers have dared what the many feared
And conquered in spite of the men who jeered
For the joys that are and the things we know
Were the dreams of the few in the long ago."

Jack Kelly was a dreamer, and he has proved that the refinement of those with meagre beginnings is the triumph of Christian civilization. He proved beyond all doubt that there is no reason why the artisan should not hold a copy of Shelley or Tennyson as well as a hammer or saw. It used to be that snobs of higher society felt that only those with a college education were interested in culture. History beams with cases like that of Jack Kelly. Carnegie fired a boiler for one dollar a week, borrowed books from the library and educated himself. Franklin, out of school at the age of ten, was one of the greatest speakers of the world in his day and spoke eight languages. President Andrew Jackson's wife taught him to read and write after they were married.

As president of Atlantic City Race Track, one of his many sidelines, Jack has put many of his revolutionary ideas to work. He cut down the first tree at Atlantic City Race Track, and has since proudly watched it grow into one of the finest racing plants in the United States.

Jack has never owned a race horse in his life, but has always been a racing fan. He tries to operate a faultless track, as clean as possible. In a race a couple of seasons ago, there was a bad start as the favorite didn't come out of the starting gate, even though the gate opened. Those who had bet on the favorite were wild. They threatened to tear down the grandstand. Sensing trouble, Jack walked out into the infield, grabbed ahold of the public address microphone, and calmly said, "Take it easy, folks. You will get your money back." Then he returned $74,000, unheard of in racing circles!

Jack has constantly kept the public's interest uppermost in

his mind. He started Ladies Day and was the first to print the "morning line" on programs.

He felt that the fans had been shoved around at tracks too much, and did something about that, too. He personally sat in twenty-one different types of seats before ordering those finally installed at Atlantic City Race Track. He said that the patron should be comfortable, and insisted that there be thirty-nine inches between rows of seats.

Always progressive and imaginative, Jack envisioned turf-racing as part of his original plan. He believed in racing on the turf because a horse spends his first two years galloping in the meadows.

Jack called his board of directors together for a meeting one afternoon and announced that Atlantic City Race Track needed something novel to attract more paying customers.

"What do you suggest?" one of the directors asked.

"Racing on turf," said Jack.

The stockholders stiffened, but Jack battled their apprehensions with facts.

"Hialeah is using it, and doing very well," said Jack. "I know it will work for us, too. We have a mile and a furlong track, same scope infield and circumference as the Florida track. Actually, we should be able to offer better turf racing because more horses are available at the time of our meeting."

Jack won his point. Turf racing was launched at Atlantic City in 1949.

One of Jack Kelly's admirers said, "They ought to erect a monument to that guy." But monuments are for the dead. Jack Kelly is still very much alive and, God willing, he will remain a living monument, the most inspiring to behold.

As close as one may come to attaining immortality in the hearts and minds of men, Jack Kelly has achieved the life everlasting in that he leaves behind a vital part of himself everywhere he goes. Men have tried to express it in selecting him the greatest oarsman in U.S. history, in naming a swimming pool after him, in honoring him with sundry humanitarian awards.

I think he summed up his life best of all when, thinking about the day when he must leave this best of planets, he said philosophically:

"Life owes me nothing. I have ranged the world far and wide, and have really run the gamut. I have known great sorrow and great joy. I have had more than my share of success. My wife and children have not given me any heartaches, and I deeply appreciate that.

"Looking back today, I believe that life has a mysterious way of balancing the books. Success and prosperity can sometimes hurt a person more than adversity.

"Without that first abysmal disappointment in 1920, I might never have achieved success. Beethoven once said, when he lay near death, that of all the experiences he had in his career, if he had to give up all the memories but one he would keep his disappointments, because they taught him most.

"In my Will, I can only give my family material things, but if I had the choice of giving them worldly goods or character, I would give them character. The reason for that is if a person has character he will get worldly goods, because character is loyalty, honesty, ability, sportsmanship and, I hope, a sense of humor.

"So when the hour comes for me to shove off for greener pastures, or whatever it is on the other side of the Curtain, just remember that I do it unafraid—and, if you must know, a little curious.

"However, life still has much to offer me. If anything, my role in society gets busier—and richer with meaning. I truly hope my next sixty-seven years are as full as the last sixty-seven."

Amen.

Index

Albert, King, 106, 112, 113
Angyal, Joe, 191

Baker, General, 214
Beatty, Terence, 179
Beethoven, 224
Bell, Bert, 74-78
Beresford, Jack, 103-08
Bonner, Father, 123, 124
Brando, Marlon, 210
Britt, Jimmy, 55
Brown, Judge John Dudley, 40, 41
Bryan, William Jennings, 40
Burk, Joe, 195
Burke, Sr., Jackie, 67
Burke, Jr., Jackie, 67
Butt, Alfred, 51
Byrne, Ed, 64, 65

Campbell, Jim, 206
Carnegie, Dale, 222
Clarey, Eddie, 67
Clark, S. R., 111
Clark, Jim, 135
Cobb, Ty, 11
Conant, Howell, 200
Considine, Bob, 152
Cooper, Gary, 203
Corrigan, Wrong Way, 177
Costello, Grandfather, 44-46, 50, 82, 95
Costello, John, 22
Costello, Paul, 101, 103, 105, 106, 109-13, 116, 117, 120, 181
Crosby, Bing, 208, 211

Davis, George, 158, 159, 171, 215

Davis, Meg, 218-19
Dempsey, Jack, 8, 9, 11, 91
Dewar, Lord, 54
Dibble, Bob, 97, 98, 101
Dorando, M., 54, 55
Dorias, Mike, 75, 76
Doyle, Mike, 125, 126
Drain, Sims, 190
Dressler, Marie, 44, 45
Dubois, Theo, 179, 180, 191, 192

Earle, George, 132
Ederle, Gertrude, 91
Edison, Thomas, 32
Egan, Wallace, 182
Eisenhower, President Ike, 154, 177
Elder, Ruth, 177
Eliot, George, 128

Farley, Elliot, 63
Farley, James, 131
Feller, Bobby, 11
Fields, W. C., 50
Flanagan, Joe, 196-98
Ford, Godfrey, 198
Ford, Henry, 32
Ford, John, 204
Franklin, Benjamin, 222
Freeman, Mary, 144, 205-07, 215
Fronsdal, Carl, 170-73, 193
Forshaw, B., 55

Gable, Clark, 213
Gallagher, Art, 165
Gallagher, V. J., 111
Gallico, Paul, 98-101
Garland, Judy, 208
Girard, Frank, 45
Gleason, Jackie, 65
Grakelow, Charles, 187
Grange, Red, 11, 91
Graves, E. D., 111
Guest, Edgar, 221

Hadfield, R., 105
Hambelton, Lady, 173
Hapgood, Bill, 122, 123
Harriman, Averill, 195
Hayes, Johnny, 54, 55
Heffernan, Mike, 54, 55
Hitler, Adolph, 147
Hoffman, Ed, 120
Holden, William, 209, 213-14

Jackson, Andrew, 222
Jacomini, V. V., 111
Johnson, Russell, 93, 94
Johnston, D. J., 111
Jones, Bobby, 11, 91
Jones, Jennifer, 207
Jordan, W. C., 111

Kelly, Ann, 14, 15, 88, 114
Kelly, Ann (*Kell's daughter*), 207

Kelly, Bill, 113, 114
Kelly, Charles, 5, 15, 30, 83, 124
Kelly, Colin, 164
Kelly, Father David F., 113
Kelly, Elizabeth, 15, 35, 44, 60, 88, 101, 124
Kelly, George, 5, 15, 30-32, 35, 44, 60, 73, 80, 81, 83-85, 87-89, 124, 200-02
Kelly, Grace (*Aunt*), 15, 24, 25, 28, 35, 44, 69, 101, 123, 124
Kelly, Grace, 7, 89, 125, 137, 157-60, 171, 175, 180, 182, 199-220
Kelly, John, 3, 4
Kelly, John B. (Jack), 4-11, 14-19, 22, 30-34, 44, 46, 57-69, 72-88, 91-101, 103-17, 119-35, 138-45, 147-55, 159, 161, 166, 168-75, 177-82, 184, 186-88, 194-96, 200-04, 207, 211-18, 220-24
Kelly, John B. (*Kell*), 5, 8, 10, 11, 137-45, 157-59, 161, 163-88, 194-99, 205-07, 212, 215, 218-19
Kelly, John Henry, 13, 15-17, 19-24, 34, 44, 64, 67
Kelly, Lizanne, 137, 157-61, 171, 175, 180, 182, 199, 215-18
Kelly, Margaret Majer, 10, 11, 72, 73, 88, 101, 115-17, 119, 120, 123, 127, 129, 138-40, 147, 148, 157, 158, 160, 171, 175, 180, 182, 183, 186, 211, 213-15, 218-20
Kelly, Mary (*Mother*), 15-31, 34, 35, 44, 58, 59, 67, 69, 74, 80, 84, 86-89, 92, 94-96, 108, 113, 115, 116, 123, 124
Kelly, Mary (*Daughter*), 15, 35, 88, 127
Kelly, Patrick Henry, 4, 14, 26, 30-32, 71, 83, 85, 87, 92, 93, 120, 124
Kelly, Peggy, 123, 137, 157-61, 171, 180, 182, 184, 199, 212, 215, 218-20
Kelly, Sue, 207
Kelly, Walter, 5, 15, 16, 28, 30-32, 35-40, 42-55, 57, 73, 80, 84, 85, 87-89, 124, 135, 175, 179, 203
King, C. W., 111
Kocerka, Teodore, 205
Kraus, Dr. Hans, 154

Lauder, Harry, 35
LeVine, Donald, 215-17
Lindbergh, Charles, 177
Lipton, Sir Thomas, 54

Massey, Raymond, 202
McCarthy, Pat, 65-67
McCoy, Kid, 55
McGovern, Terry, 34
McGraw, John J., 32
McIntyre, Joe, 191
McIlvaine, Charles J., 181, 185
McKenzie, R. Tate, 186

McLemore, Henry, 152
Moore, E. P., 111, 112
Moore, Thomas, 22
Muldoon, Billy, 92
Muller, Jake, 62, 105
Murphy, Hughie, 36
Murphy, Mike, 166

Neilan, Paddy, 64, 65, 117, 198
Nelson, Battling, 34
Nino, Al, 144, 145

O'Dwyer, William, 176, 178
O'Keefe, Tommy, 145
Otley, Jess, 85, 86, 120, 125

Pegler, Westbrook, 8
Perlberg, William, 211
Pinches, J. H., 165
Pollock, Ed, 194
Prendergast, Twin, 68

Rainier, Prince, 7, 218
Ratoff, Gregory, 204
Ray, Ted, 67
Rogers, Will, 48, 49
Roosevelt, Franklin D., 135, 148, 149
Roosevelt, Theodore, 32
Rose, Ralph, 55
Rowe, Tony, 212
Ruhlin, Gus, 34
Ruth, Babe, 11, 91
Ryan, Pat, 113

Samuel, Bernard, 176-78, 180, 183, 186
Sanborn, A. R., 111
Sande, Earle, 91
Scholes, Lou, 97
Scholes, Nat, 97
Seaton, George, 208
Sephariades, Jean, 166
Sharkey, Tom, 34
Sheppard, Fred, 32, 34, 61, 108
Shor, Toots, 68, 69
Smith, Charlie, 81
Stidolph, Dave, 57
Sullivan, James E., 195
Sullivan, John L., 32

Tilden, Bill, 91
Tjukalov, Josef, 205
Truscott, Frank, 180, 182, 183, 186, 188
Tunney, Gene, 9, 11

Washington, General George, 4, 55, 113

Weismuller, Johnny, 91
Whalen, Grover, 176, 178
Whitlock, Brand, 106
Whitney, Harry, 195
Williams, Percy, 44, 45
Williams, Tommy, 190
Wills, Helen, 91
Wilson, S. Davis, 133
Wilson, Woodrow, 73, 162
Wood, Mervin, 212